HAMMOND
Historical World Atlas

A collection of maps illustrating the most significant periods and events in history from the dawn of civilization to the present day.

Contents

HAMMOND World Atlas Corporation
Revised 2003 Edition © 2000 Hammond World Atlas Corporation

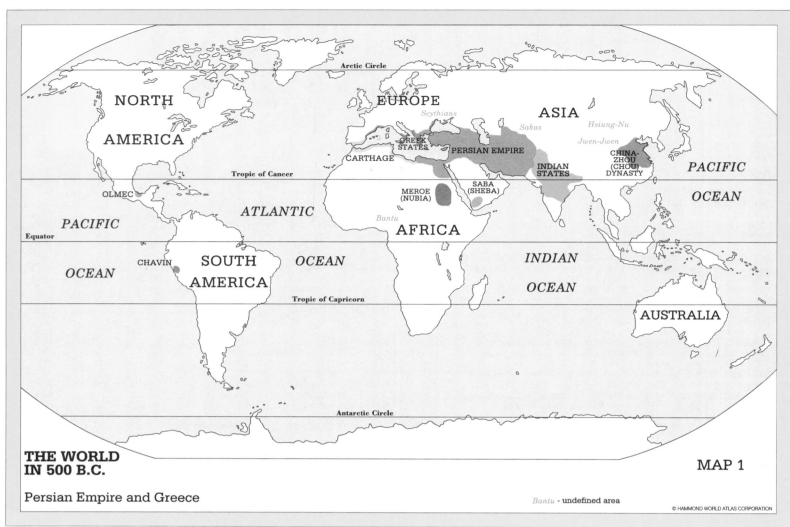

THE WORLD IN 500 B.C.

Persian Empire and Greece

MAP 1

Bantu - undefined area

© HAMMOND WORLD ATLAS CORPORATION

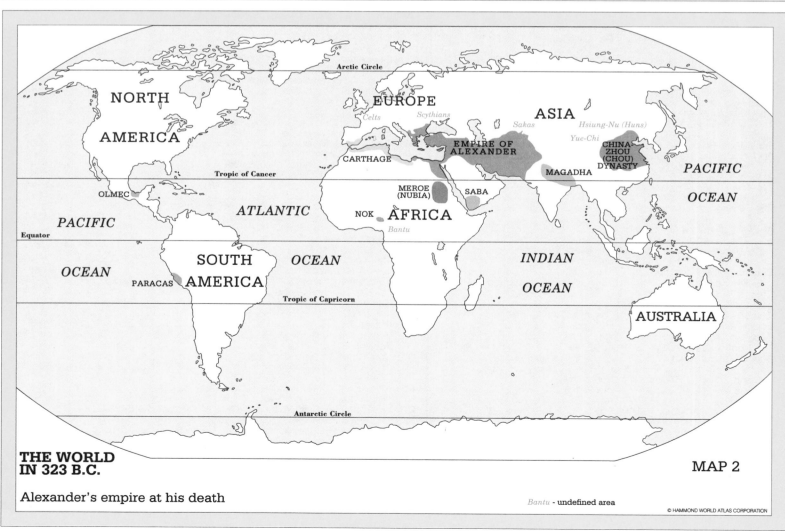

THE WORLD IN 323 B.C.

Alexander's empire at his death

MAP 2

Bantu - undefined area

© HAMMOND WORLD ATLAS CORPORATION

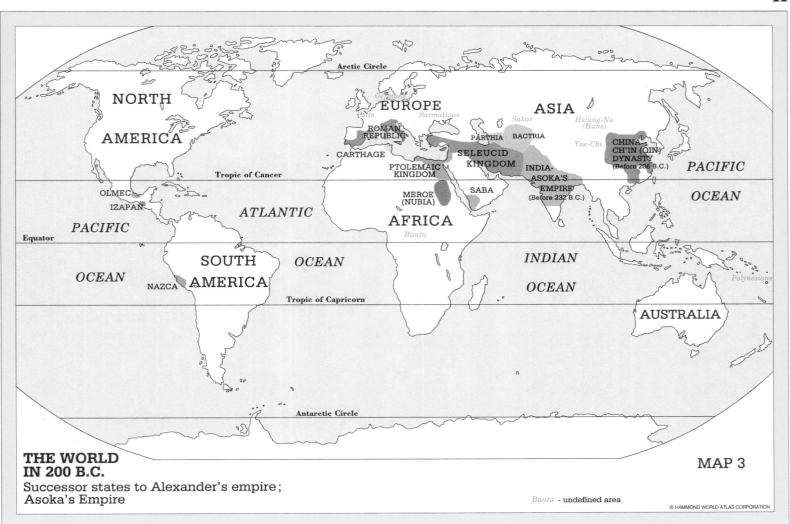

**THE WORLD
IN 200 B.C.**

Successor states to Alexander's empire;
Asoka's Empire

MAP 3

Bantu - undefined area

© HAMMOND WORLD ATLAS CORPORATION

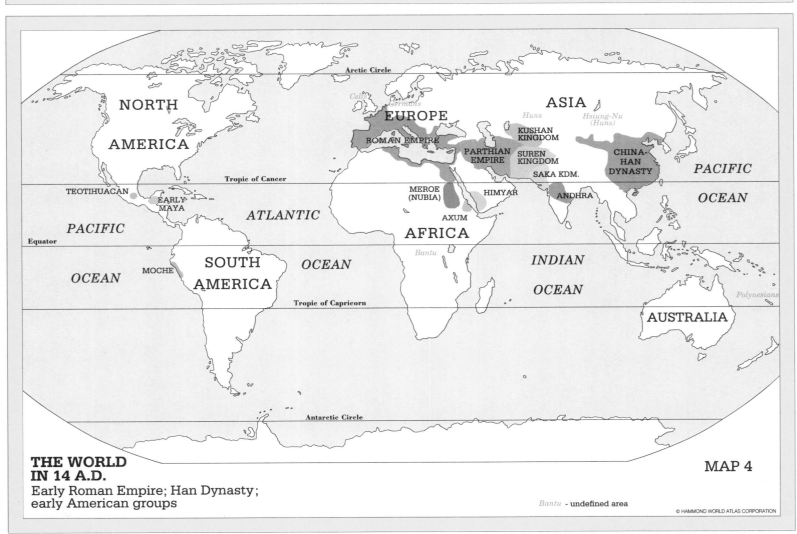

**THE WORLD
IN 14 A.D.**

Early Roman Empire; Han Dynasty;
early American groups

MAP 4

Bantu - undefined area

© HAMMOND WORLD ATLAS CORPORATION

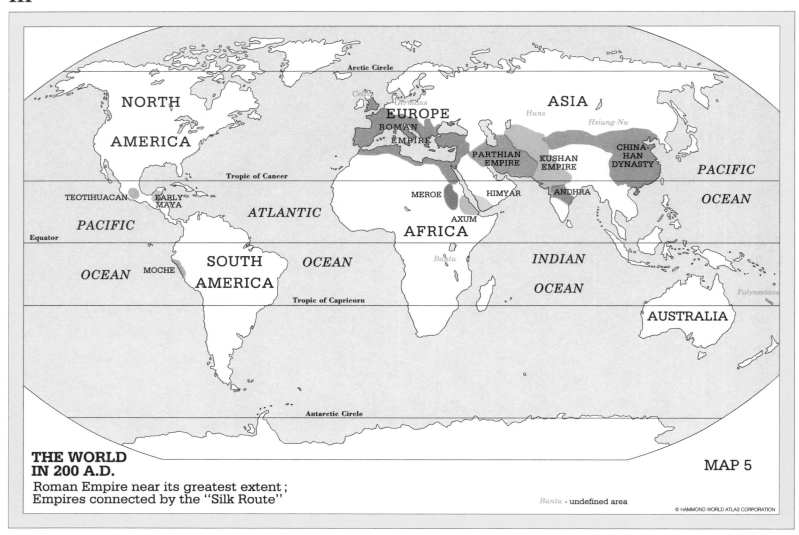

**THE WORLD
IN 200 A.D.**

MAP 5

Roman Empire near its greatest extent;
Empires connected by the "Silk Route"

Bantu - undefined area

© HAMMOND WORLD ATLAS CORPORATION

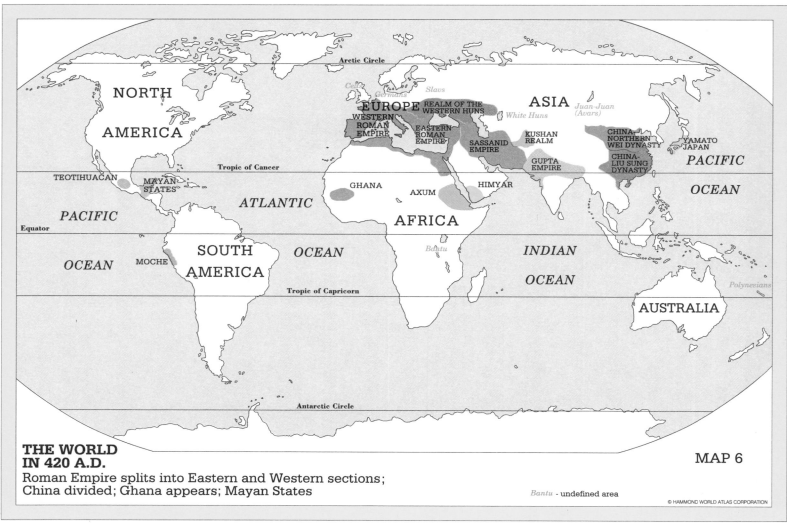

**THE WORLD
IN 420 A.D.**

MAP 6

Roman Empire splits into Eastern and Western sections;
China divided; Ghana appears; Mayan States

Bantu - undefined area

© HAMMOND WORLD ATLAS CORPORATION

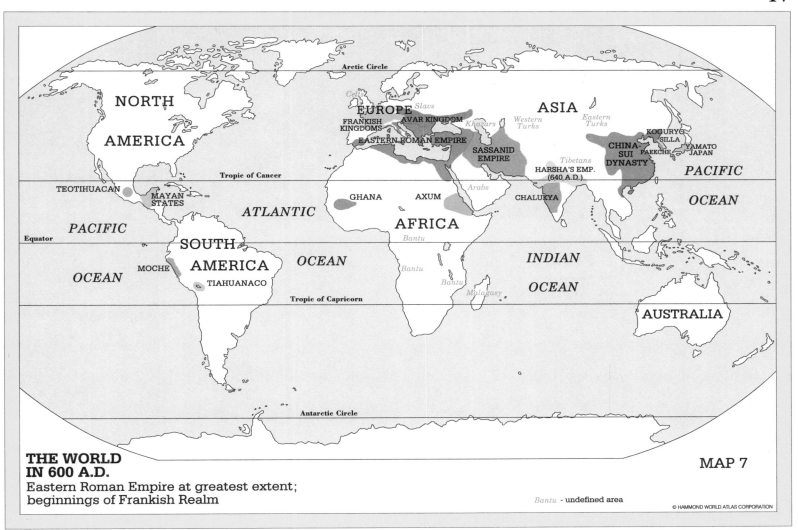

THE WORLD IN 600 A.D.

Eastern Roman Empire at greatest extent;
beginnings of Frankish Realm

Bantu - undefined area

MAP 7

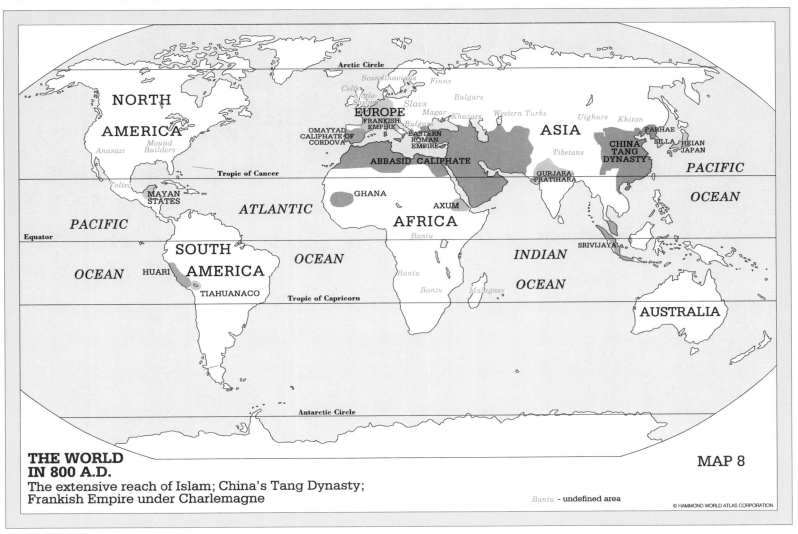

THE WORLD IN 800 A.D.

The extensive reach of Islam; China's Tang Dynasty;
Frankish Empire under Charlemagne

Bantu - undefined area

MAP 8

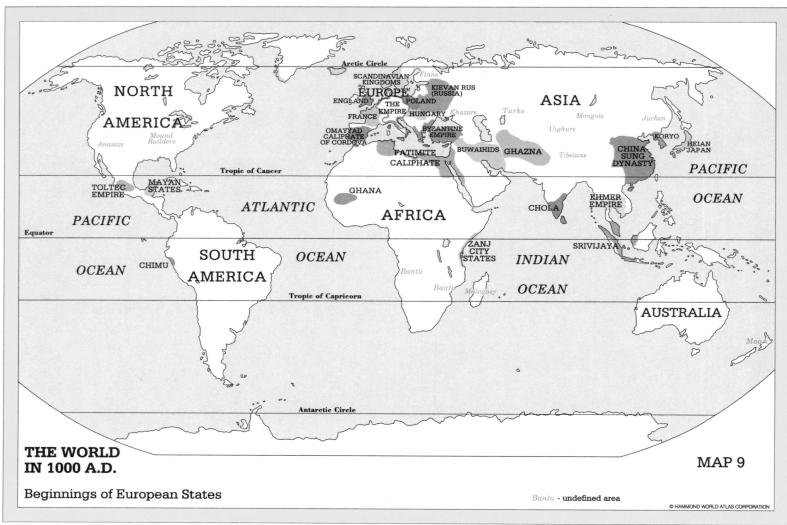

THE WORLD IN 1000 A.D.

Beginnings of European States

MAP 9

Bantu - undefined area

© HAMMOND WORLD ATLAS CORPORATION

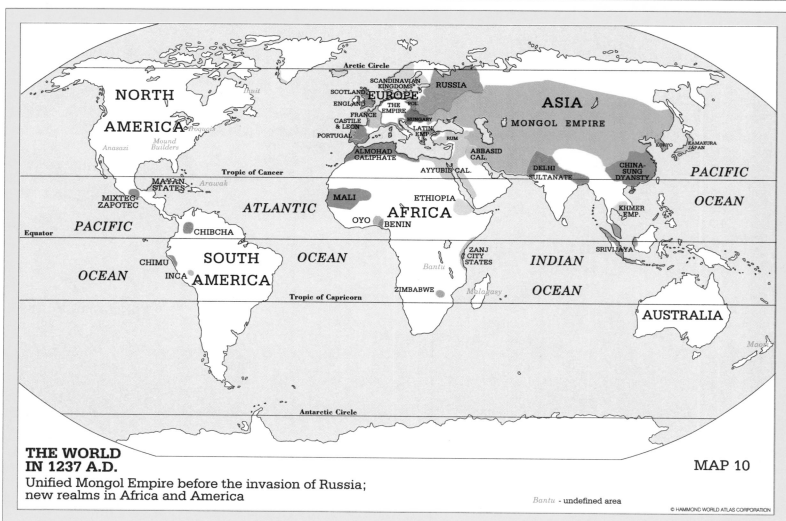

THE WORLD IN 1237 A.D.

Unified Mongol Empire before the invasion of Russia; new realms in Africa and America

MAP 10

Bantu - undefined area

© HAMMOND WORLD ATLAS CORPORATION

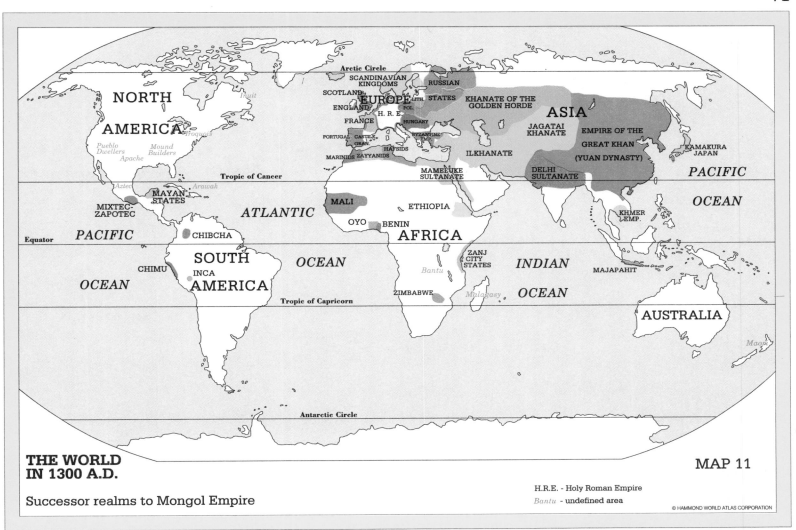

**THE WORLD
IN 1300 A.D.**

MAP 11

Successor realms to Mongol Empire

H.R.E. - Holy Roman Empire

Bantu - undefined area

© HAMMOND WORLD ATLAS CORPORATION

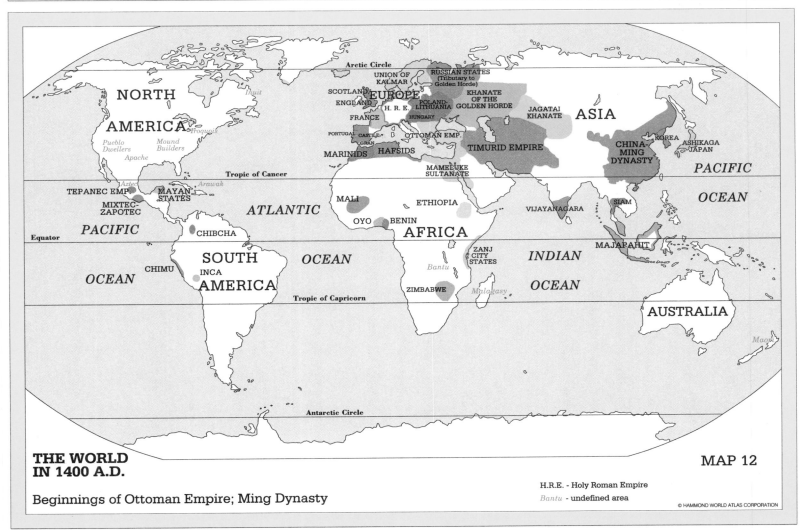

**THE WORLD
IN 1400 A.D.**

MAP 12

Beginnings of Ottoman Empire; Ming Dynasty

H.R.E. - Holy Roman Empire

Bantu - undefined area

© HAMMOND WORLD ATLAS CORPORATION

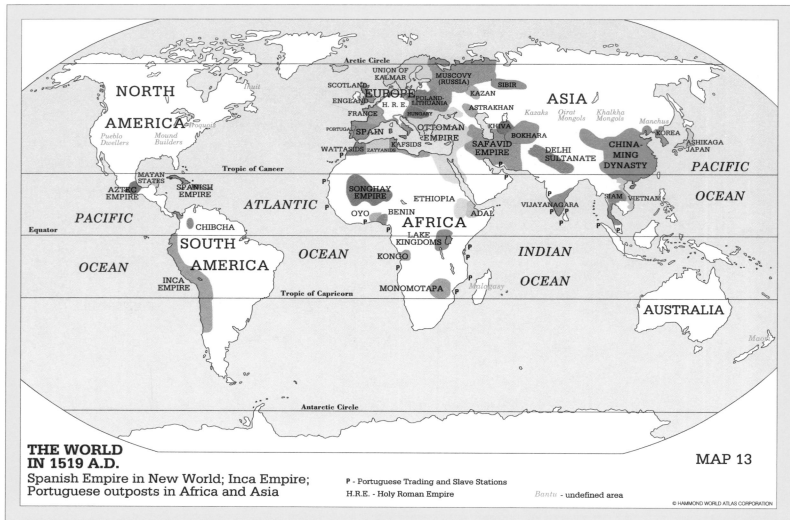

THE WORLD
IN 1519 A.D.

Spanish Empire in New World; Inca Empire;
Portuguese outposts in Africa and Asia

P - Portuguese Trading and Slave Stations

H.R.E. - Holy Roman Empire

Bantu - undefined area

MAP 13

© HAMMOND WORLD ATLAS CORPORATION

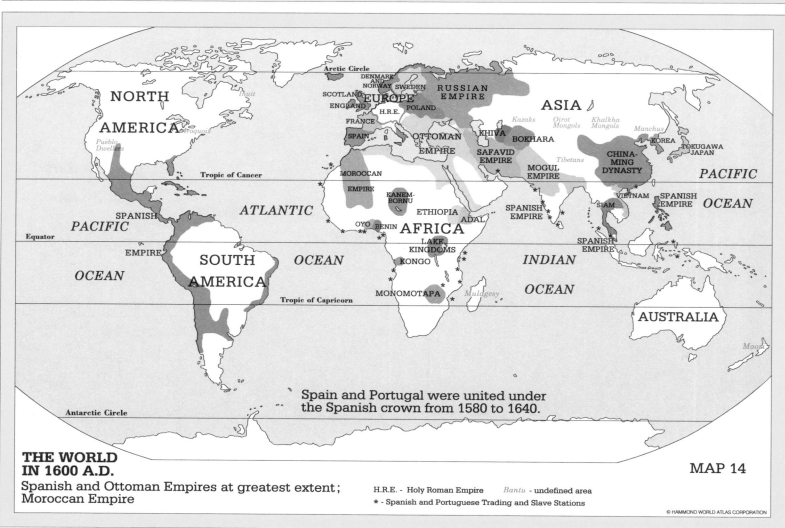

Spain and Portugal were united under
the Spanish crown from 1580 to 1640.

THE WORLD
IN 1600 A.D.

Spanish and Ottoman Empires at greatest extent;
Moroccan Empire

H.R.E. - Holy Roman Empire   *Bantu* - undefined area

* - Spanish and Portuguese Trading and Slave Stations

MAP 14

© HAMMOND WORLD ATLAS CORPORATION

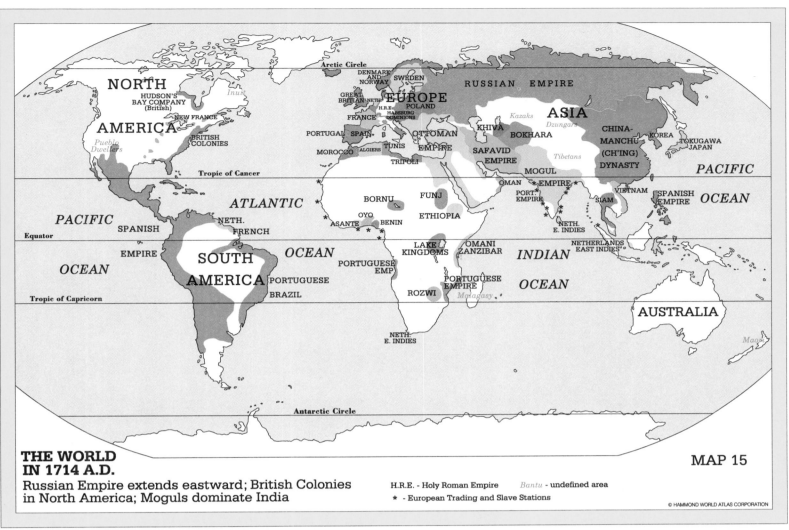

NORTH
AMERICA

HUDSON'S
BAY COMPANY
(British)

NEW FRANCE

BRITISH
COLONIES

Pueblo
Dwellers

ATLANTIC

NETH.

FRENCH

SPANISH

EMPIRE

OCEAN

PACIFIC

OCEAN

SOUTH
AMERICA

PORTUGUESE
BRAZIL

PORTUGUESE
EMP.

Arctic Circle

DENMARK
AND
NORWAY

SWEDEN

GREAT
BRITAIN

NETH.

EUROPE

POLAND

RUSSIAN EMPIRE

H.R.E.
HABSBURG
DOMINIONS

FRANCE

PORTUGAL SPAIN

MOROCCO

ALGIERS

TUNIS

TRIPOLI

OTTOMAN

EMPIRE

Kazaks

KHIVA

ASIA

Dzungars

BOKHARA

CHINA-
MANCHU
(CH'ING)
DYNASTY

KOREA

TOKUGAWA
JAPAN

SAFAVID
EMPIRE

Tibetans

MOGUL

OMAN

EMPIRE

PORT.
EMPIRE

VIETNAM

SIAM

SPANISH
EMPIRE

PACIFIC

OCEAN

NETH.
E. INDIES

BORNU

FUNJ

ASANTE

OYO

BENIN

ETHIOPIA

LAKE
KINGDOMS

OMANI
ZANZIBAR

INDIAN

NETHERLANDS
EAST INDIES

Equator

PORTUGUESE
EMP.

PORTUGUESE
EMPIRE

OCEAN

Tropic of Cancer

Tropic of Capricorn

ROZWI

Malagasy

AUSTRALIA

Maori

NETH.
E. INDIES

Antarctic Circle

**THE WORLD
IN 1714 A.D.**

Russian Empire extends eastward; British Colonies
in North America; Moguls dominate India

H.R.E. - Holy Roman Empire   *Bantu* - undefined area

* - European Trading and Slave Stations

MAP 15

© HAMMOND WORLD ATLAS CORPORATION

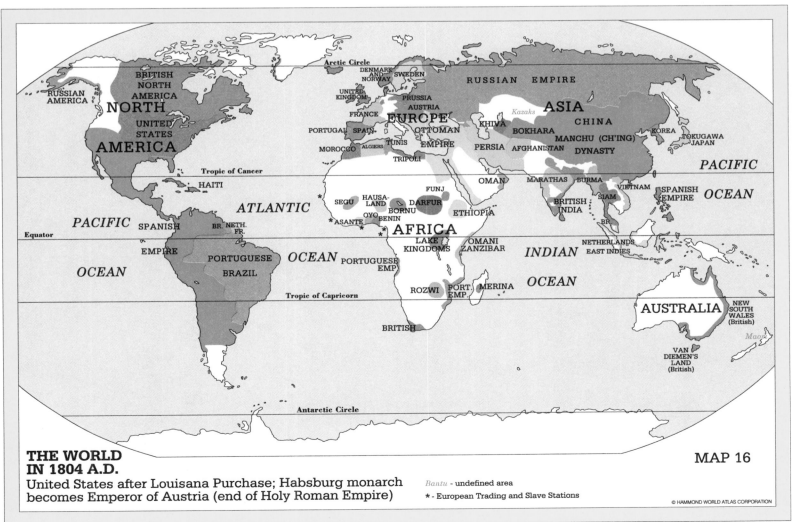

RUSSIAN
AMERICA

BRITISH
NORTH
AMERICA

NORTH

UNITED
STATES

AMERICA

PACIFIC

SPANISH

EMPIRE

OCEAN

HAITI

ATLANTIC

BR. NETH.
FR.

OCEAN

PORTUGUESE
BRAZIL

Arctic Circle

DENMARK
AND
NORWAY

SWEDEN

UNITED
KINGDOM

PRUSSIA

AUSTRIA

FRANCE

EUROPE

RUSSIAN EMPIRE

Kazaks

ASIA

CHINA

PORTUGAL SPAIN

MOROCCO

ALGIERS

TUNIS

TRIPOLI

OTTOMAN

EMPIRE

KHIVA

BOKHARA

PERSIA

AFGHANISTAN

MANCHU (CH'ING)

DYNASTY

KOREA

TOKUGAWA
JAPAN

PACIFIC

OMAN

MARATHAS

BURMA

VIETNAM

SIAM

BRITISH
INDIA

BR.

SPANISH
EMPIRE

OCEAN

SEGU

HAUSA-
LAND

FUNJ

DARFUR

BORNU

OYO

BENIN

ETHIOPIA

NETHERLANDS
EAST INDIES

ASANTE

AFRICA

LAKE
KINGDOMS

OMANI
ZANZIBAR

INDIAN

Equator

PORTUGUESE
EMP.

OCEAN

Tropic of Cancer

Tropic of Capricorn

ROZWI

PORT.
EMP.

MERINA

Maori

BRITISH

AUSTRALIA

NEW
SOUTH
WALES
(British)

VAN
DIEMEN'S
LAND
(British)

Antarctic Circle

**THE WORLD
IN 1804 A.D.**

United States after Louisana Purchase; Habsburg monarch
becomes Emperor of Austria (end of Holy Roman Empire)

Bantu - undefined area

* - European Trading and Slave Stations

MAP 16

© HAMMOND WORLD ATLAS CORPORATION

PREHISTORIC MAN

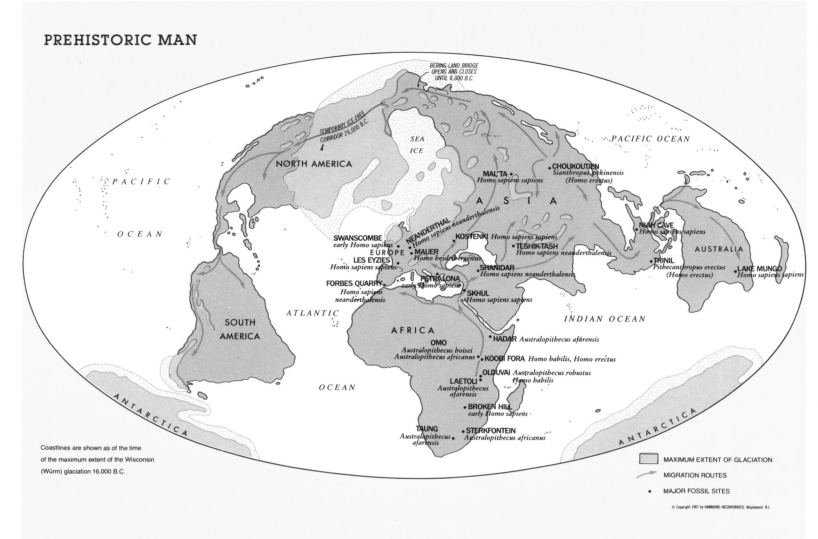

MAL'TA
Homo sapiens sapiens

CHOUKOUTIEN
Sianthropus pekinensis
(Homo erectus)

BERING LAND BRIDGE
OPENS AND CLOSES
UNTIL 8,000 B.C.

SEA
ICE

PACIFIC OCEAN

NORTH AMERICA

TEMPORARY ICE FREE
CORRIDOR 26,000 B.C.

A S I A

PACIFIC

OCEAN

NIAH CAVE
Homo sapiens sapiens

SWANSCOMBE
early Homo sapiens

NEANDERTHAL
Homo sapiens neanderthalensis

KOSTENKI Homo sapiens sapiens

TESHIK-TASH
Homo sapiens neanderthalensis

EUROPE

MAUER
Homo heidelbergensis

AUSTRALIA

LES EYZIES
Homo sapiens sapiens

SHANIDAR
Homo sapiens neanderthalensis

TRINIL
Pithecanthropus erectus
(Homo erectus)

LAKE MUNGO
Homo sapiens sapiens

FORBES QUARRY
Homo sapiens
neanderthalensis

PETRALONA
early Homo sapiens

SKHUL
Homo sapiens sapiens

ATLANTIC

INDIAN OCEAN

SOUTH
AMERICA

OCEAN

AFRICA

OMO
Australopithecus boisei
Australopithecus africanus

HADAR Australopithecus afarensis

KOOBI FORA Homo habilis, Homo erectus

OLDUVAI Australopithecus robustus
Homo habilis

OCEAN

LAETOLI
Australopithecus
afarensis

BROKEN HILL
early Homo sapiens

ANTARCTICA

TAUNG
Australopithecus
afarensis

STERKFONTEIN
Australopithecus africanus

ANTARCTICA

Coastlines are shown as of the time
of the maximum extent of the Wisconsin
(Würm) glaciation 16,000 B.C.

MAXIMUM EXTENT OF GLACIATION

MIGRATION ROUTES

MAJOR FOSSIL SITES

© Copyright 1987 by HAMMOND INCORPORATED, Maplewood, N.J.

THE SPREAD OF FARMING
AND EARLY DOMESTICATION
OF CROPS AND ANIMALS

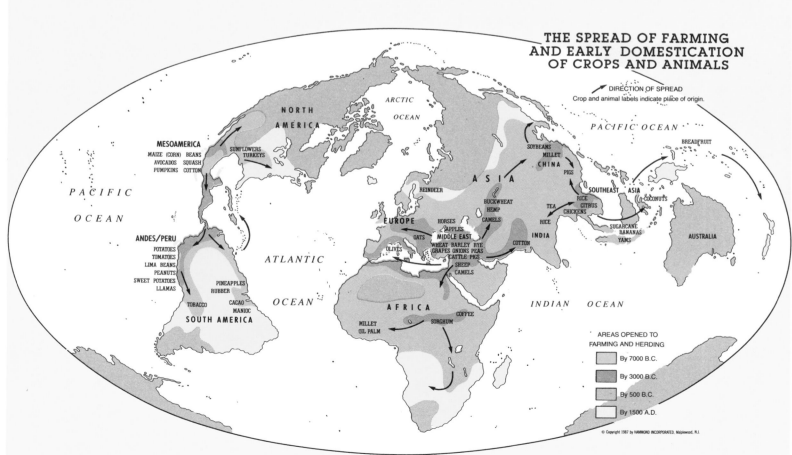

DIRECTION OF SPREAD
Crop and animal labels indicate place of origin.

ARCTIC
OCEAN

NORTH
AMERICA

PACIFIC OCEAN

MESOAMERICA
MAIZE (CORN) BEANS
AVOCADOS SQUASH
PUMPKINS COTTON

SUNFLOWERS
TURKEYS

BREADFRUIT

SOYBEANS
MILLET
CHINA

ASIA

REINDEER

PIGS

SOUTHEAST ASIA

PACIFIC

COCONUTS

OCEAN

BUCKWHEAT
HEMP
CAMELS

TEA
CITRUS
CHICKENS

RICE

EUROPE

HORSES
APPLES

RICE

ANDES/PERU
POTATOES
TOMATOES
LIMA BEANS
PEANUTS
SWEET POTATOES
LLAMAS

OATS

MIDDLE EAST
WHEAT BARLEY RYE
GRAPES ONIONS PEAS
CATTLE PIGS
SHEEP
CAMELS

INDIA

ATLANTIC

OLIVES

COTTON

SUGARCANE
BANANAS
YAMS

AUSTRALIA

PINEAPPLES
RUBBER

TOBACCO

CACAO
MANIOC

OCEAN

SOUTH AMERICA

AFRICA

COFFEE

INDIAN OCEAN

MILLET
OIL PALM

SORGHUM

AREAS OPENED TO
FARMING AND HERDING

By 7000 B.C.

By 3000 B.C.

By 500 B.C.

By 1500 A.D.

© Copyright 1987 by HAMMOND INCORPORATED, Maplewood, N.J.

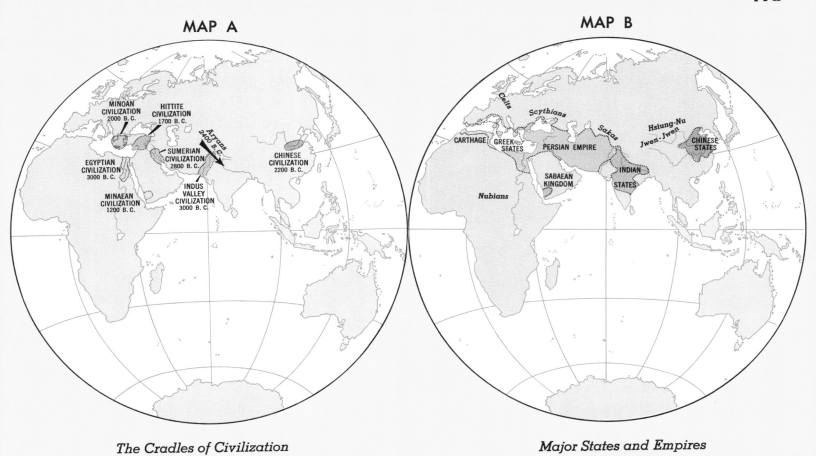

MAP A

MINOAN
CIVILIZATION
2000 B.C.

HITTITE
CIVILIZATION
1700 B.C.

Aryans
2400 B.C.

EGYPTIAN
CIVILIZATION
3000 B.C.

SUMERIAN
CIVILIZATION
2800 B.C.

CHINESE
CIVILIZATION
2200 B.C.

MINAEAN
CIVILIZATION
1200 B.C.

INDUS
VALLEY
CIVILIZATION
3000 B.C.

*The Cradles of Civilization
3000-1000 B.C.*

MAP B

Celts

Scythians

Sakas

Hsiung-Nu
Jwen-Jwen

CARTHAGE
GREEK
STATES
PERSIAN EMPIRE

CHINESE
STATES

SABAEAN
KINGDOM

INDIAN
STATES

Nubians

*Major States and Empires
in 500 B.C.*

MAP C

MAYAN
STATES

Huns

KOKURYO

JAPAN

Germans
Slavs

White
Huns

WEI EMPIRE

SUNG
EMPIRE

K. OF
MULAVARMAN

WESTERN
ROMAN

Berbers

EASTERN
EMPIRE

KUSHAN
STATES

PROME

FUNAN

LANGKASUKA

Hindus

KINGDOM
OF GHANA

SASSANID
EMPIRE

GUPTA
EMPIRE

Hindus

TARUMA

HIMYARITIC
KINGDOM

PALLAVA

CEYLON

AXUMITE
KINGDOM

*Major States and Empires
in 400 A.D.*

MAP D

Spaniards

JAPAN

TIDORE

KOREA

TERNATE

MING
DYNASTY
OF CHINA

BRUNEI

MACASSAR

Russians

ANNAM

AZTEC
EMPIRE
(1519)

BURMA

SIAM

MATARAM

MAYAN STATES
(1527)

French

RUSSIAN
EMPIRE

BUKHARA

Moslems

ATJEH

English

MOGUL
EMPIRE

Spaniards

OTTOMAN
EMPIRE

PERSIA

Spaniards

INCA
EMPIRE
(1533)

MOROCCO

BORNU

Portuguese

SONGHOY
EMPIRE

HAUSA

BAGUIRMI

DARFUR

ETHIOPIA

Dutch

Portuguese

Dutch

*The Expansion
of Western Civilization
1600 A.D.*

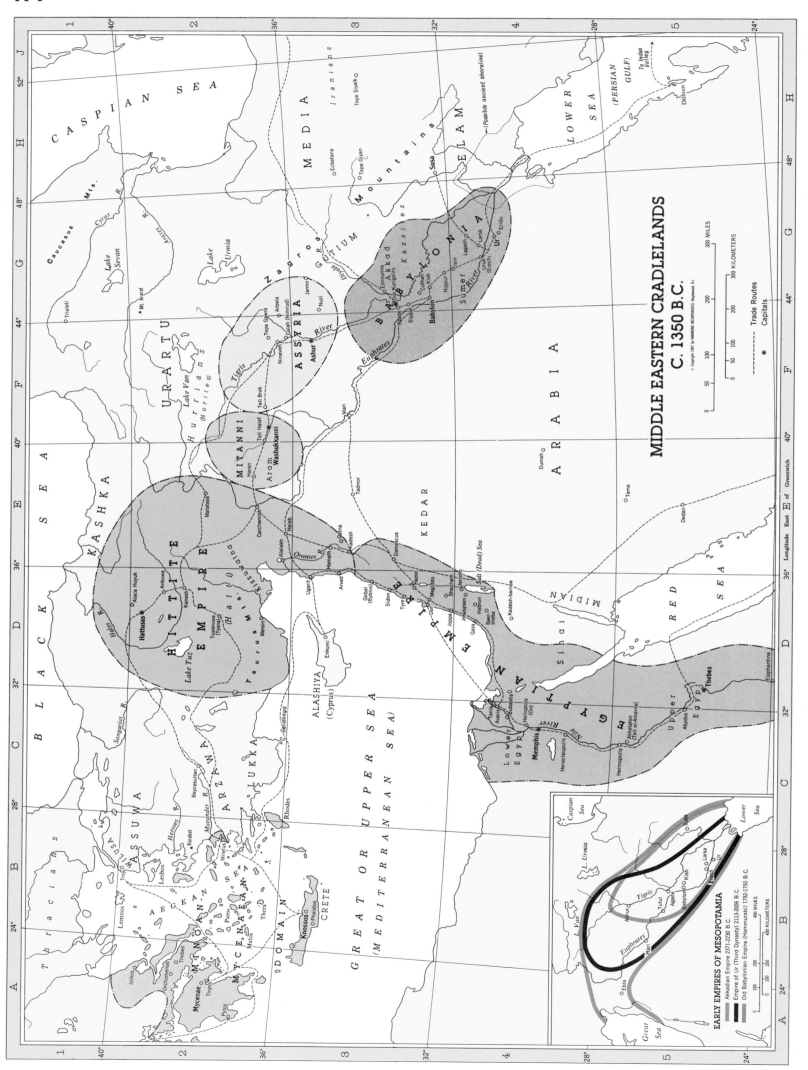

MIDDLE EASTERN CRADLELANDS
C. 1350 B.C.

© Copyright 1987 by HAMMOND INCORPORATED Maplewood, N.J.

--------- Trade Routes
● Capitals

0 50 100 200 300 MILES
0 50 100 200 300 KILOMETERS

EARLY EMPIRES OF MESOPOTAMIA

	Akkadian Empire 2371-2230 B.C.
	Empire of Ur (Third Dynasty) 2113-2006 B.C.
	Old Babylonian Empire (Hammurabi) 1792-1750 B.C.

0 100 200 400 MILES
0 100 200 400 KILOMETERS

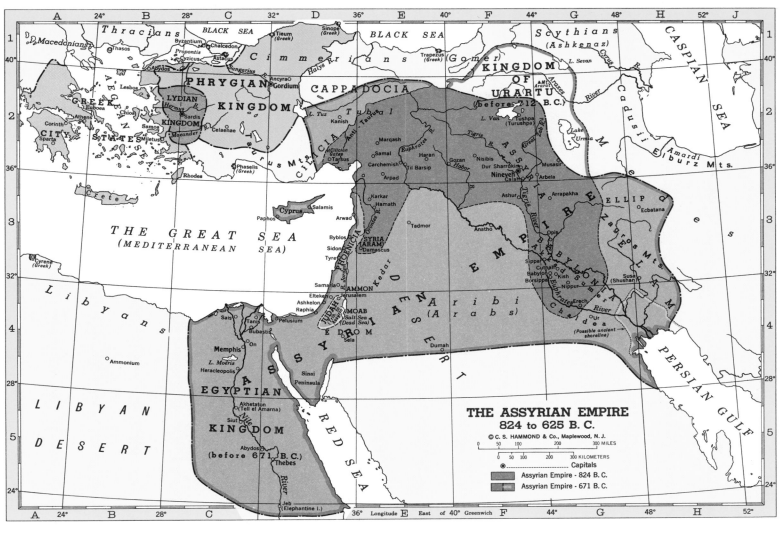

THE ASSYRIAN EMPIRE
824 to 625 B.C.

© C. S. HAMMOND & Co., Maplewood, N. J.

| 0 | 50 | 100 | 200 | 300 MILES |
| 0 | 50 | 100 | 200 | 300 KILOMETERS |

○ Capitals

Assyrian Empire - 824 B. C.

Assyrian Empire - 671 B. C.

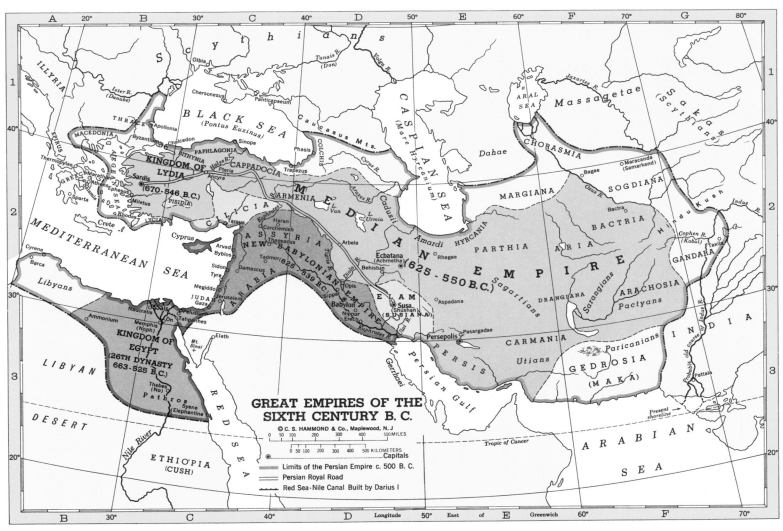

GREAT EMPIRES OF THE
SIXTH CENTURY B.C.

© C. S. HAMMOND & Co., Maplewood, N. J.

| 0 | 50 | 100 | 200 | 300 | 400 | 500 MILES |
| 0 | 50 | 100 | 200 | 300 | 400 | 500 KILOMETERS |

○ Capitals

Limits of the Persian Empire c. 500 B. C.

Persian Royal Road

Red Sea-Nile Canal Built by Darius I

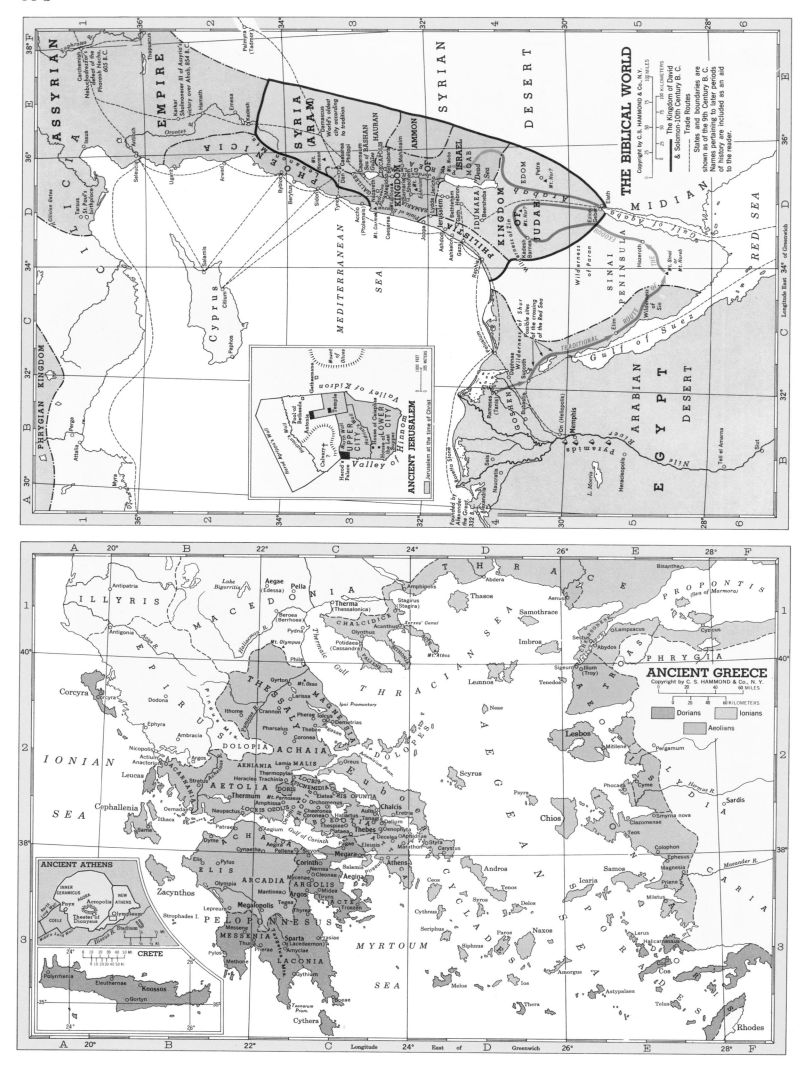

THE BIBLICAL WORLD

Copyright by C.S. HAMMOND & Co., N.Y.

The Kingdom of David & Solomon-10th Century B.C.

Trade Routes

States and boundaries are shown as of the 9th Century B.C. Names pertaining to later periods of history are included as an aid to the reader.

ANCIENT JERUSALEM
Jerusalem at the time of Christ

ANCIENT GREECE

Copyright by C.S. HAMMOND & Co., N.Y.

Dorians

Ionians

Aeolians

ANCIENT ATHENS

CRETE

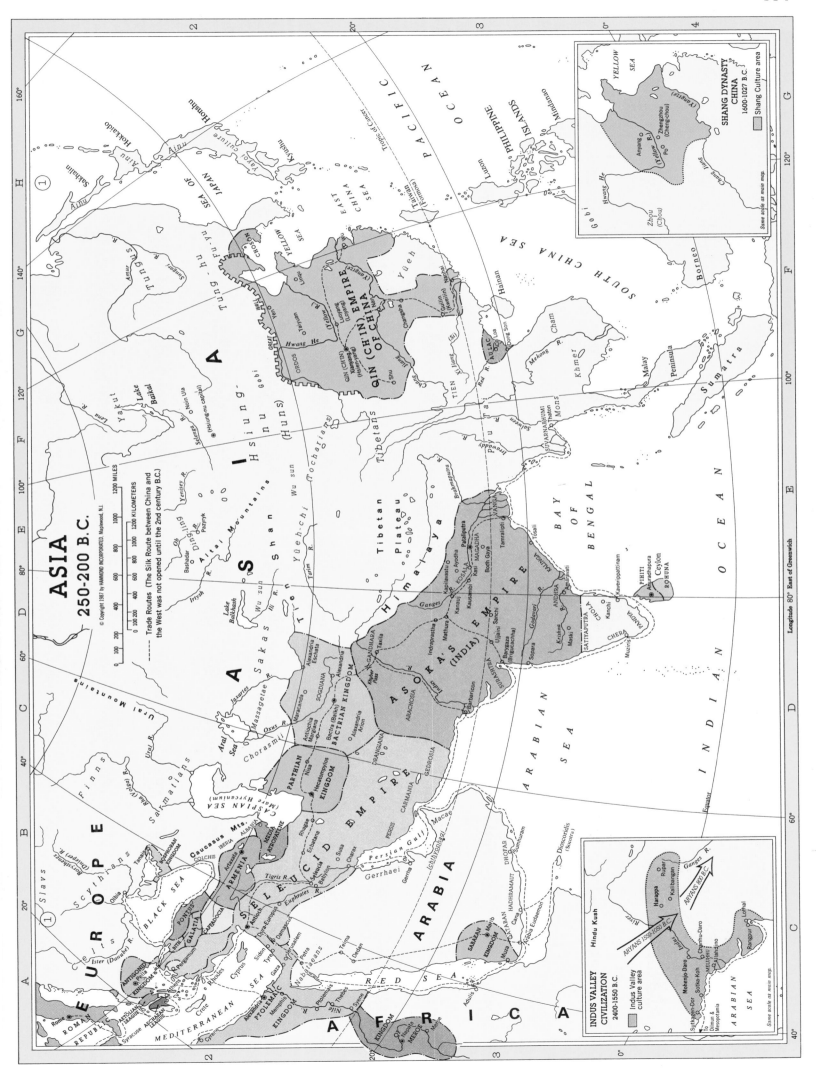

ASIA
250-200 B.C.

© Copyright 1987 by HAMMOND INCORPORATED, Maplewood, N.J.

—— Trade Routes (The Silk Route between China and
the West was not opened until the 2nd century B.C.)

0 100 200 400 600 800 1000 1200 MILES
0 100 200 400 600 800 1000 1200 KILOMETERS

SHANG DYNASTY CHINA
1600-1027 B.C.
Shang Culture area

YELLOW SEA

Anyang   Zhengzhou (Cheng-chou)
Yellow R.   Po
Gobi
Zhou (Chou)   Chang Jiang (Yangtze)
Hwang He
Same scale as main map.

INDUS VALLEY CIVILIZATION
2400-1550 B.C.
Indus Valley culture area

Hindu Kush
Harappa   Rupar
Kalibangan   Ganges R.
ARYANS 800 B.C.
ARYANS 1550-1050 B.C.
Mohenjo-Daro   Chanhu-Daro
Sutkagen-Dor   Sotka-Koh   Kalibangan
To Dilmun & Mesopotamia   Amri   Allahdino   Rangpur   Lothal
ARABIAN SEA
Same scale as main map.

Longitude 80° East of Greenwich

EUROPE

Slavs
Scythians
Borysthenes (Dnieper) R.
Rha (Volga) R.
Tanais
Sarmatians
Finns
Ural Mountains
Ural R.
Aral Sea
Jaxartes R.
Massagetae
Lake Balkhash
Ili R.
Wu-sun
Sakas
Tien Shan
Yüeh-chi
Wu sun
Altai Mountains
Dingling
Bashadar
Pazyryk
Irtysh R.
Ob
Yenisey R.
Selenga
Noin Ula
(Hsiung-nu capital)
Lake Baikal
Yakut
Lena
Amur
Tunguses
Sungari
Ussuri
Ainu
Sakhalin
Ainu
Hokkaido
Honshu
Ainu
Yayoi culture area
Tun-hu-Sun
SEA OF JAPAN
Kyushu
CHOSON
YELLOW SEA

A S I A

H s i u n g - n u   (H u n s)
ORDOS
Qin (CHIN)
Xianyang (Hsienyang)
Kanyang
Luoyang (Loyang)
QIN (CH'IN) EMPIRE
OF CHINA
Great Wall
Hwang He (Yellow R.)
Yen
Taiyuan
Shu
Changsha
Chu
Guilin (Kweilin)
Yüeh
Nanhai
X Jiang (Si)
Red R.
AU LAC
Loa
Dong Son
TIEN
EAST CHINA SEA
Hainan
PHILIPPINE ISLANDS
Luzon
Mindoro
Mindanao
PACIFIC OCEAN

Tibetans
Tibetan Plateau
Tarim R.
Tochariyo (Tocharians)
Yüeh-chi
Himalaya
Ganges
GANDHARA
Taxila
Khyber Pass
Indraprastha
Mathura
Kapilavastu
Ayodhya
KOSALA
Kanauj
Kausambi
Kasi
MAGADHA
Pataliputra
Bodh Gaya
VANGA
Tamralipti
Brahmaputra
Irrawaddy
Salween
SUVARNABHUMI
Thaton
Mons
Khmer
Mekong R.
Cham
Malay Peninsula
Borneo
Sumatra
SOUTH CHINA SEA

ASOKAS (INDIA)
Ujjain
Sanchi
Barygaza (Brigukachha)
ANDHRA
Godavari
Krishna
Amaravati
KALINGA
Tosali
BAY OF BENGAL
Tamralipti
Sopara
Maski
SATYAPUTRA
CHERA
Kanchi
CHOLA
Muziris
Kaveripattinam
PANDYA
PIHITI
Anuradhapura
Ceylon
ROHUNA
INDIAN OCEAN

A S I A

PARTHIAN KINGDOM
Nisa
Hecatompylos
Rhagae
CASPIAN SEA
(Mare Hyrcanium)
Chorasmii
Oxus R.
Maracanda
SOGDIANA
Alexandria Eschata
Alexandria
Antiochia Margiana
Bactra (Balkh)
BACTRIAN KINGDOM
Alexandria Arion
DRANGIANA
ARACHOSIA
GEDROSIA
CARMANIA
Alexandria

SELEUCID EMPIRE
PERSIS
Ecbatana
Susa
Charax
PARTHIA
Persian Gulf
Gerrhaei
Gerra
Macae
Ichthyophagi
Persepolis
Pasargadae

Caucasus Mts.
COLCHIS
IBERIA
ALBANIA
ARMENIA
MEDIA ATROPATENE
MEDIA
BOSPORAN KINGDOM
Olbia
Black Sea
PONTUS
GALATIA
CAPPADOCIA
Tarsus
Antioch
Seleucia
Dura-Europus
Damascus
Sidon
Tyre
Gaza
Jerusalem
Babylon
Seleucia
Tigris
Euphrates
NABATAEANS
Petra

MEDITERRANEAN SEA
Cyrene
Crete
Rhodes
Cyprus
ANTIGONID KINGDOM
Pella
ACHAEAN LEAGUE
AETOLIAN LEAGUE
Sparta
Syracuse
ROMAN REPUBLIC
Rome

PTOLEMAIC KINGDOM
Alexandria
Memphis
Thebes
Syene
Nile
MEROS
Napata
Meroe

ARABIA
RED SEA
Teima
Dedan
Yathrib
Mecca
SABAEAN KINGDOM
Marib
Muza
Cana
Arabia Eudaemon
DHOFAR
HADHRAMAUT
Sumhuram
Sumuram
Moscha
Dioscoridis (Socotra)
ARABIAN SEA
Adulis

A F R I C A

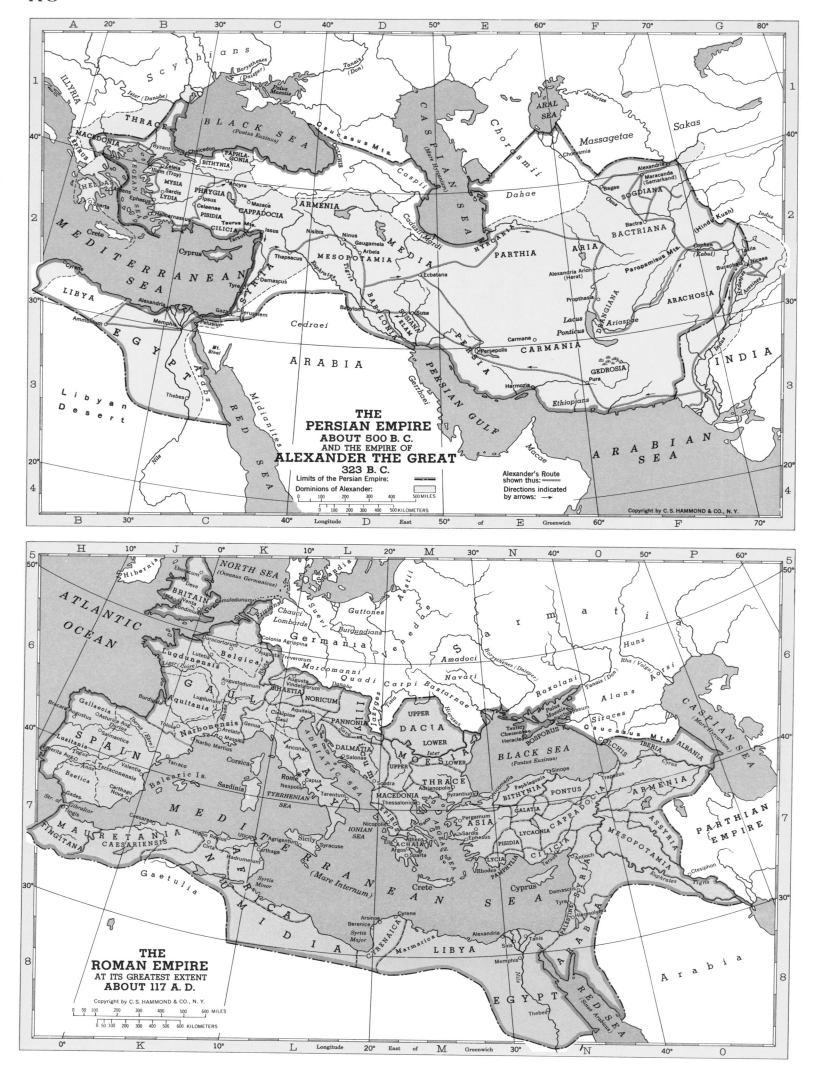

THE PERSIAN EMPIRE
ABOUT 500 B.C.
AND THE EMPIRE OF
ALEXANDER THE GREAT
323 B.C.

Limits of the Persian Empire: ——————
Dominions of Alexander:

Alexander's Route shown thus: ——————
Directions indicated by arrows: →

Copyright by C. S. HAMMOND & CO., N.Y.

THE
ROMAN EMPIRE
AT ITS GREATEST EXTENT
ABOUT 117 A.D.

Copyright by C. S. HAMMOND & CO., N.Y.

ANCIENT ITALY
ITALIA, LIGURIA, VENETIA, GALLIA-CISALPINA, HISTRIA, SICILIA & CORSICA
Before the time of Augustus

Copyright by C.S. HAMMOND & CO., N.Y.

Roman Colonies, thus: ------ Ostia
Greek Colonies, thus: ---- SYRACUSAE (G)
Carthaginian Colonies, thus: ···· Eryx (C)
Dotted lines show the Modern shore line

THE FORUM CAPITOLIUM and PALATIUM

1. Templum Saturni
2. Templum Concordiae
3. Scalae Gemoniae
4. Carcer (Tullianum)
5. Senaculum
6. Graecostasis
7. Rostra
8. Templum Jani

IMPERIAL FORA

1. Scalae Gemoniae
2. Templum Vespasiani
3. Porticus Deorum Consentium
4. Equus Caesaris
5. T. Castoris et Pollucis
6. Templum Divi Julii
7. Arcus Augusti
8. Arcus Titi
9. Templum Antonini et Faustinae

ROME
Under the Emperors

1. Templum Jovis Capitolini
2. Arx
3. Forum Romanum
4. Templum Aesculapii
5. Forum Trajani
6. Forum Augusti
7. Porta Carmentalis
8. Arcus Septimii Severi
9. Arcus Constantini
10. Arcus Titi
11. Arcus Claudii
12. Arcus Tiberii
13. Arcus Gallieni
14. Arcus Marci Aurelii
15. Arcus Diocletiani
16. Porta Flumentara
17. Templum Mercurii
18. Theatrum Marcelli

REGIONES AUGUSTI

I. Porta Capena
II. Caelimontium
III. Isis et Serapis
IV. Templum Pacis
V. Esquiliae
VI. Alta Semita
VII. Via Lata
VIII. Forum Romanum
IX. Circus Flaminius
X. Palatium
XI. Circus Maximus
XII. Piscina Publica
XIII. Aventinus
XIV. Trans Tiberim

ROME
In the time of the Republic

EURASIA
c.100 A.D.
Trade Routes .....

© Copyright 1987 by Hammond Incorporated, Maplewood, N.J.

THE KNOWN WORLD

Areas shown in yellow were known to the Romans or Chinese.

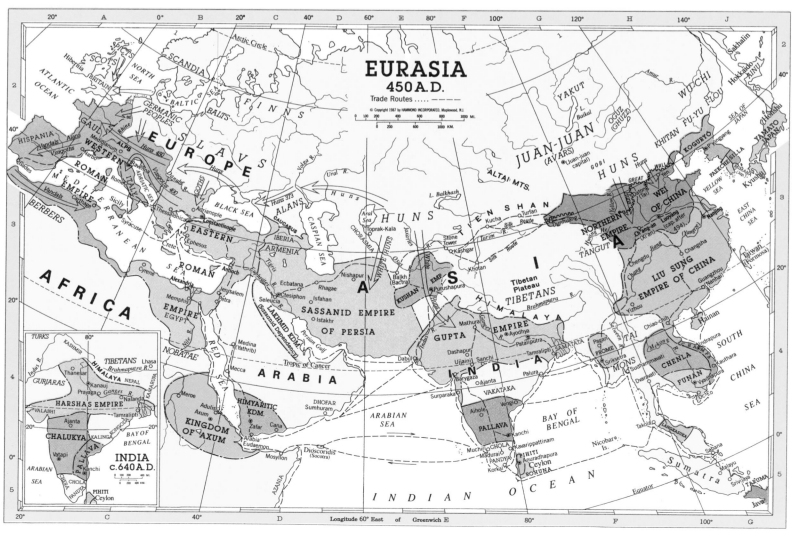

EURASIA
450 A.D.
Trade Routes .....

© Copyright 1987 by Hammond Incorporated, Maplewood, N.J.

INDIA c.640 A.D.

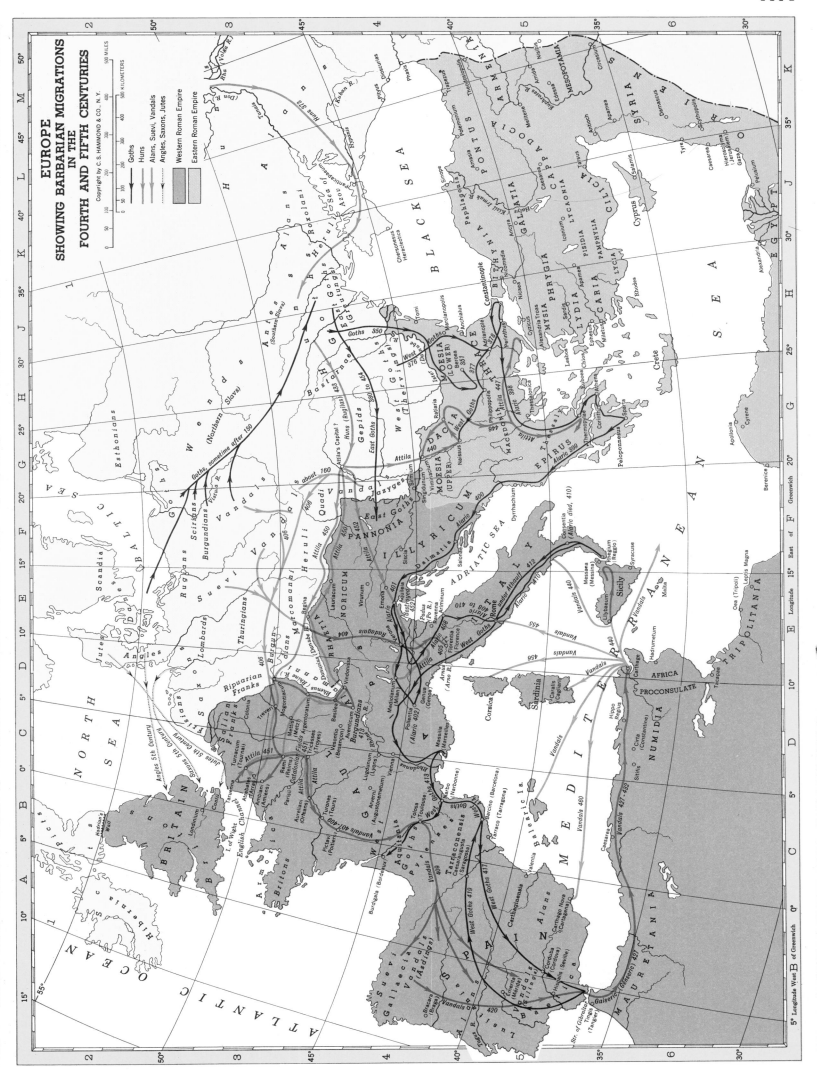

EUROPE
SHOWING BARBARIAN MIGRATIONS
IN THE
FOURTH AND FIFTH CENTURIES

Copyright by C. S. HAMMOND & CO., N.Y.

500 MILES

500 KILOMETERS

Goths
Huns
Alans, Suevi, Vandals
Angles, Saxons, Jutes
Western Roman Empire
Eastern Roman Empire

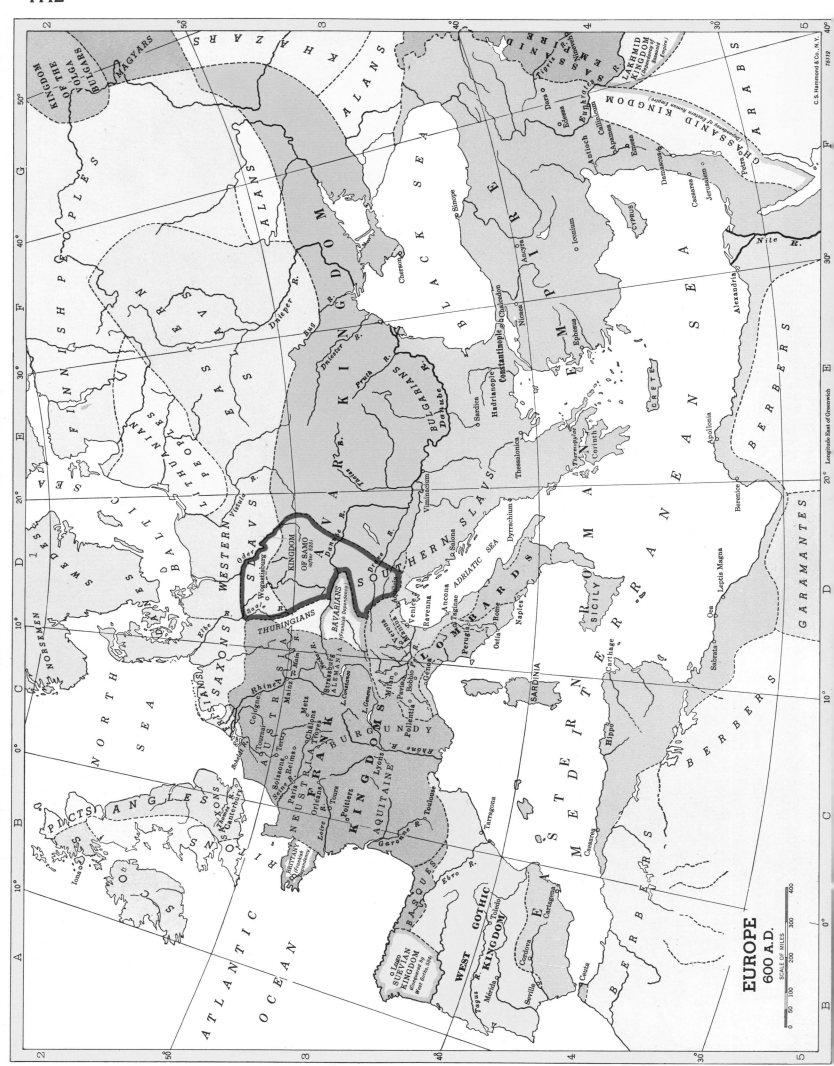

EUROPE

600 A.D.

SCALE OF MILES

0 50 100 200 300 400

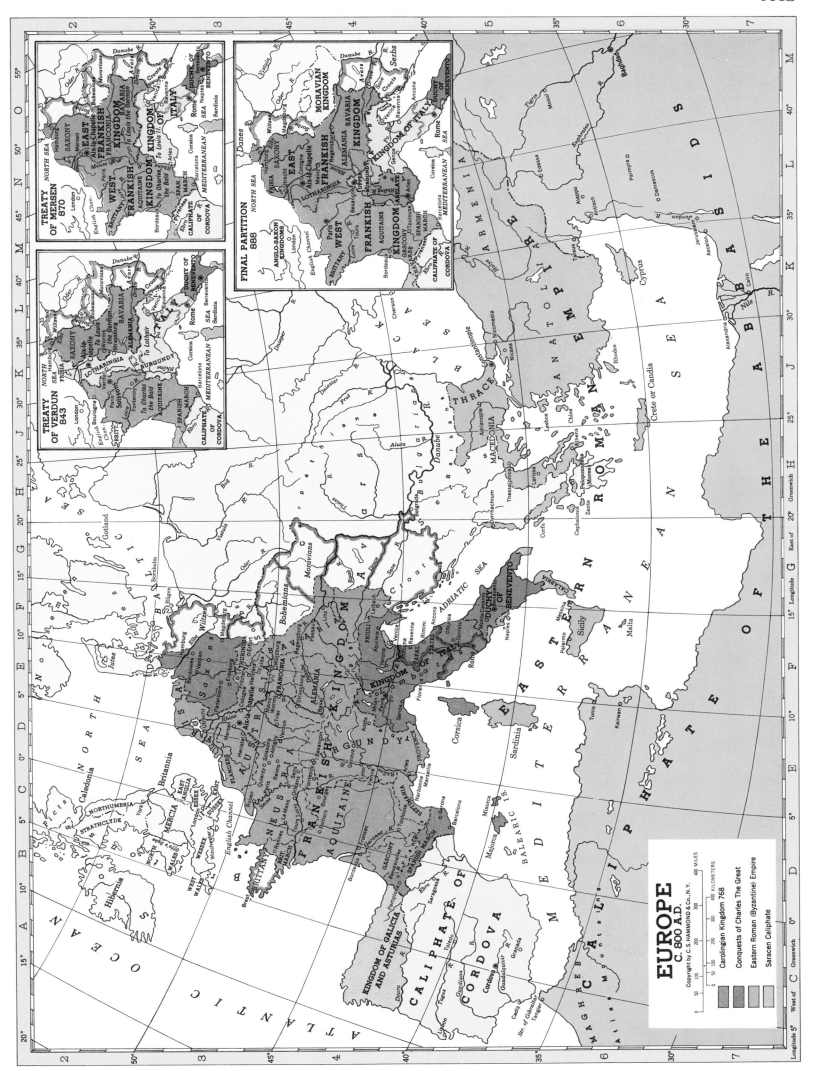

TREATY OF MERSEN 870

TREATY OF VERDUN 843

FINAL PARTITION 888

EUROPE
C. 800 A.D.

Copyright by C. S. HAMMOND & Co., N.Y.

Carolingian Kingdom 768

Conquests of Charles The Great

Eastern Roman (Byzantine) Empire

Saracen Caliphate

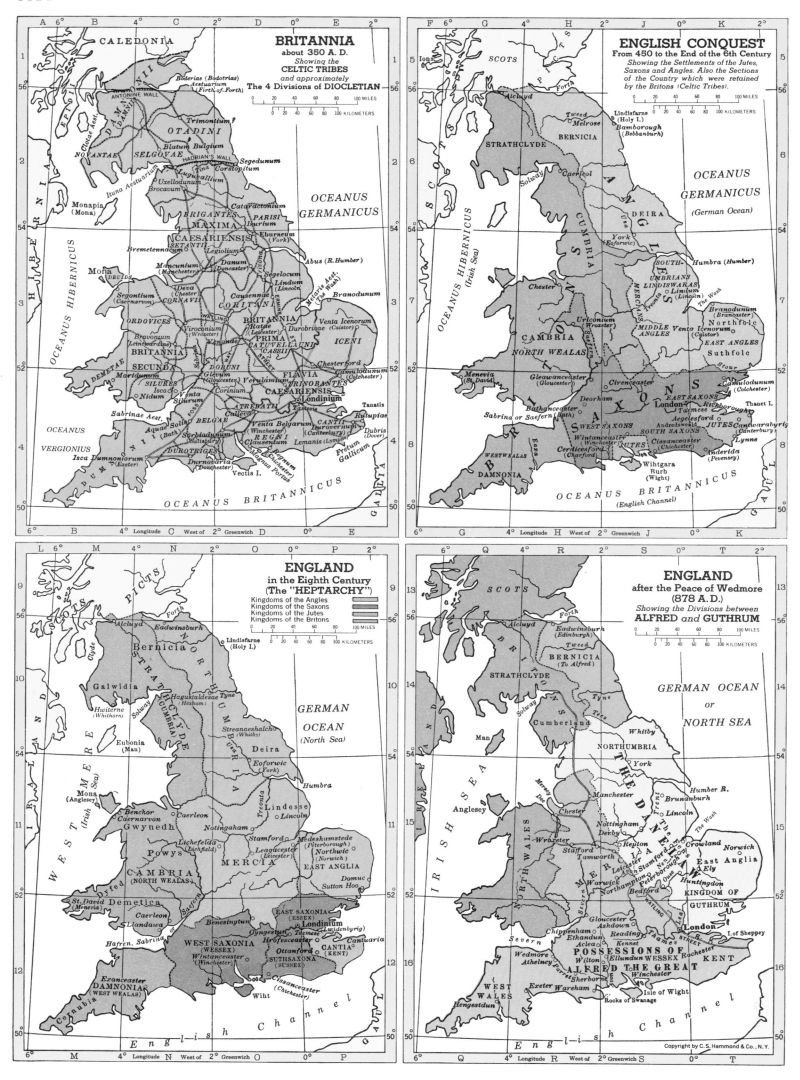

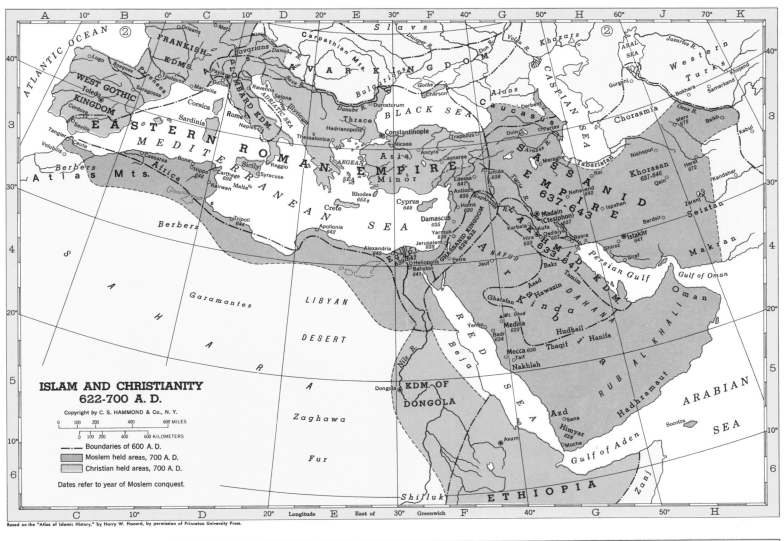

ISLAM AND CHRISTIANITY
622-700 A.D.

Copyright by C. S. HAMMOND & Co., N. Y.

0 100 200 400 600 MILES
0 100 200 400 600 KILOMETERS

— · — Boundaries of 600 A.D.
▓ Moslem held areas, 700 A.D.
░ Christian held areas, 700 A.D.

Dates refer to year of Moslem conquest.

Based on the "Atlas of Islamic History," by Harry W. Hazard, by permission of Princeton University Press.

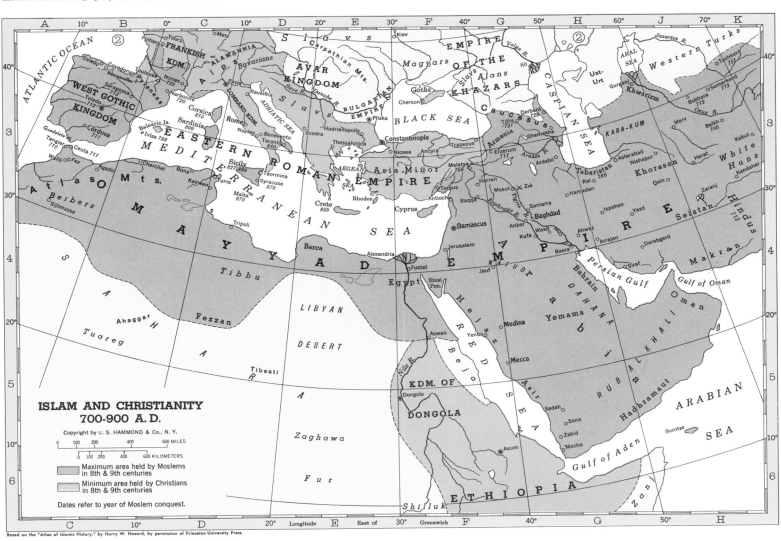

ISLAM AND CHRISTIANITY
700-900 A.D.

Copyright by C. S. HAMMOND & Co., N. Y.

0 100 200 400 600 MILES
0 100 200 400 600 KILOMETERS

▓ Maximum area held by Moslems in 8th & 9th centuries
░ Minimum area held by Christians in 8th & 9th centuries

Dates refer to year of Moslem conquest.

Based on the "Atlas of Islamic History," by Harry W. Hazard, by permission of Princeton University Press.

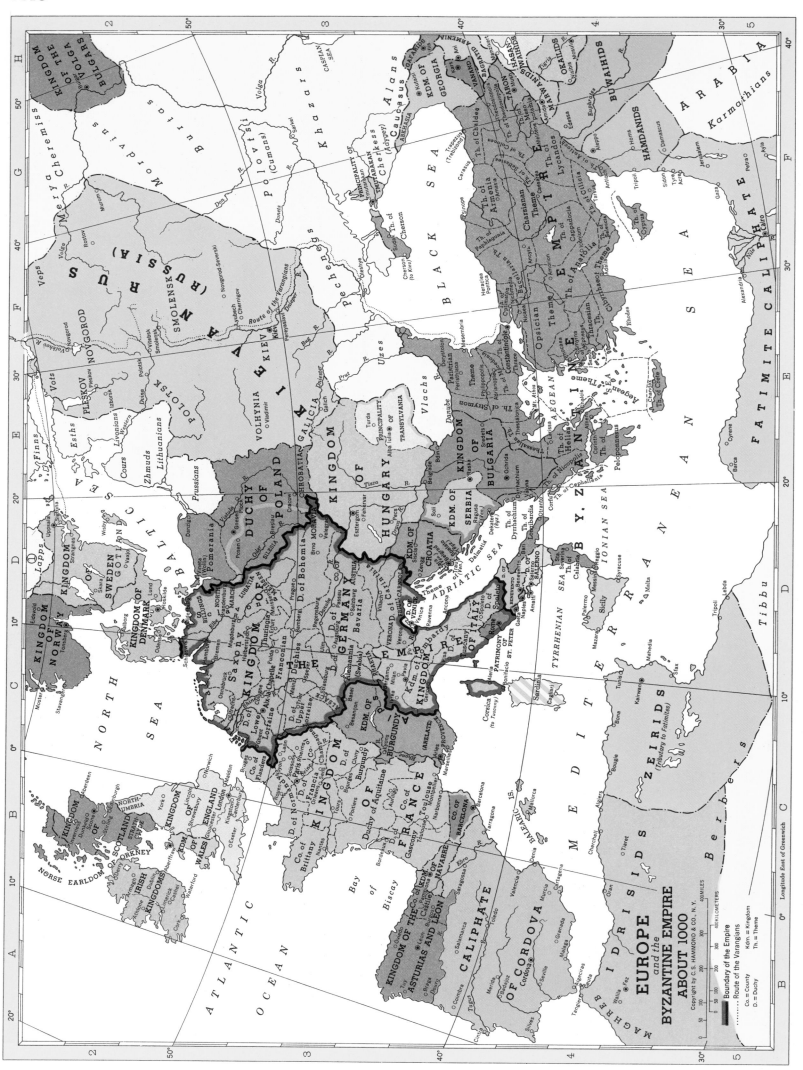

EUROPE
and the
BYZANTINE EMPIRE
ABOUT 1000

Copyright by C.S. Hammond & Co., N.Y.

Boundary of the Empire
Route of the Varangians

Co.= County   Kdm.= Kingdom
D.= Duchy   Th.= Theme

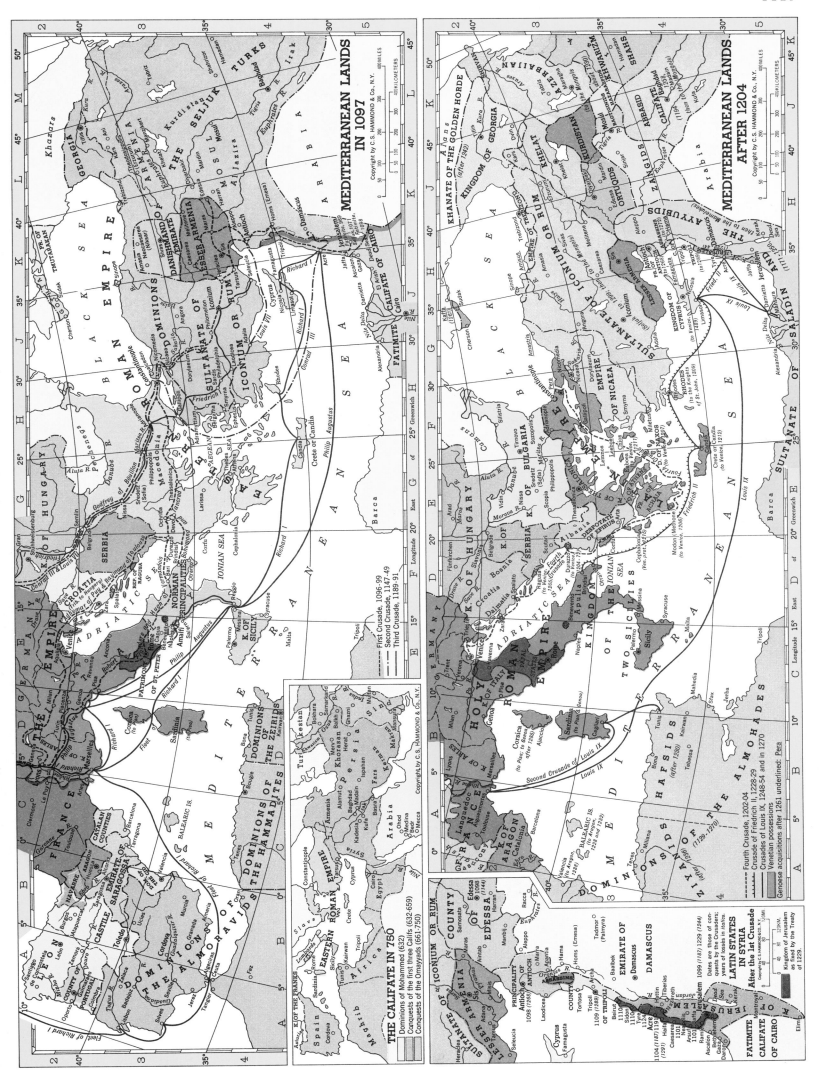

MEDITERRANEAN LANDS IN 1097

Copyright by C.S. HAMMOND & Co., N.Y.

First Crusade, 1096-99
Second Crusade, 1147-49
Third Crusade, 1189-91

THE CALIFATE IN 750

Dominions of Mohammed (632)
Conquests of the first three Califs (632-659)
Conquests of the Omayyads (661-750)

MEDITERRANEAN LANDS AFTER 1204

Copyright by C.S. HAMMOND & Co., N.Y.

Fourth Crusade, 1202-04
Crusade of Friedrich II, 1228-29
Crusades of Louis IX, 1248-54 and in 1270
Venetian possessions
Genoese acquisitions after 1261 underlined: Pera

LATIN STATES IN SYRIA
After the 1st Crusade

Dates are those of conquests by the Crusaders; years of losses in italics.

Kingdom of Jerusalem as fixed by the Treaty of 1229.

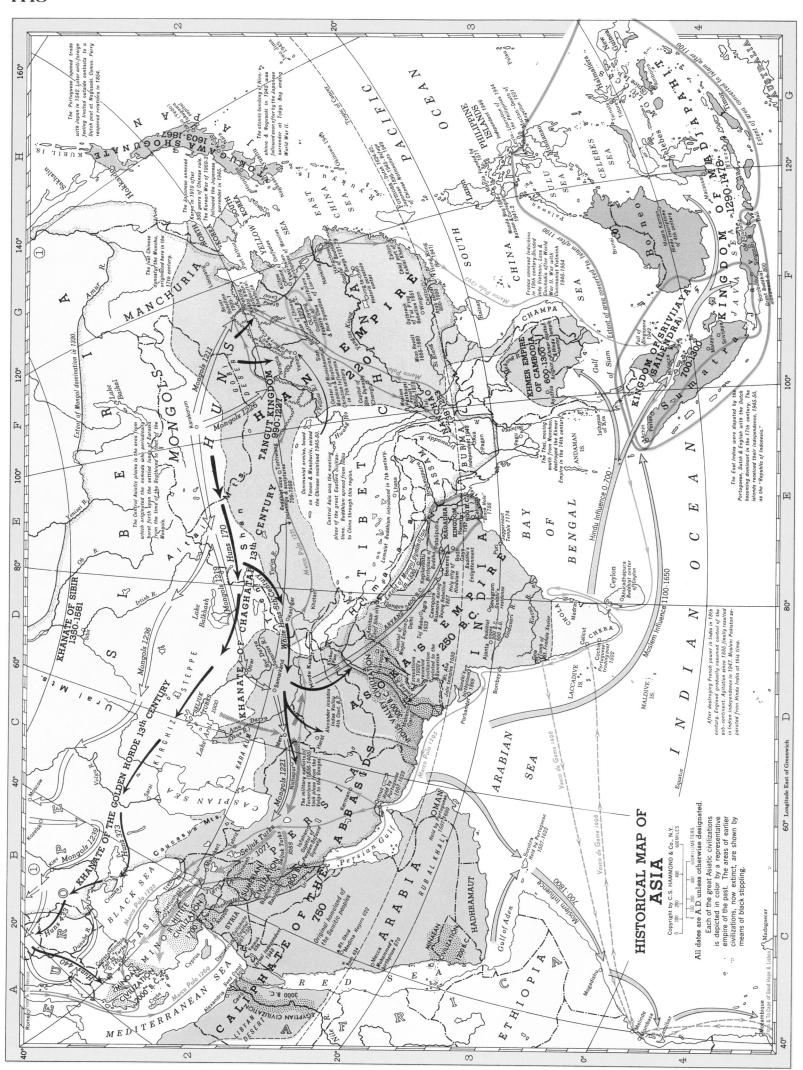

HISTORICAL MAP OF ASIA

Copyright by C.S. HAMMOND & Co., N.Y.

All dates are A.D. unless otherwise designated.

Each of the great Asiatic civilizations is depicted in color by a representative empire of the past. The areas of earlier civilizations, now extinct, are shown by means of black stippling.

EUROPE
c. 1200 A.D.

Copyright by C. S. HAMMOND & Co., N. Y.

— Boundary of the Empire
• Cities of the Lombard League
English Possessions in France in 1200
English Possessions in France in 1223
English Possessions in France in 1328

GREENLAND

Gardar

(To Trondjem)

Same scale as main map

ECCLESIASTICAL MAP OF
EUROPE
c. 1300 A. D.

0   100   200   300   400 MILES

0   100   200   300   400 KILOMETERS

Archbishoprics
Bishoprics
Monasteries
Universities

The Archepiscopal provinces are colored

Longitude   West   0°   East   of   Greenwich

C.S. HAMMOND & CO., N.Y.

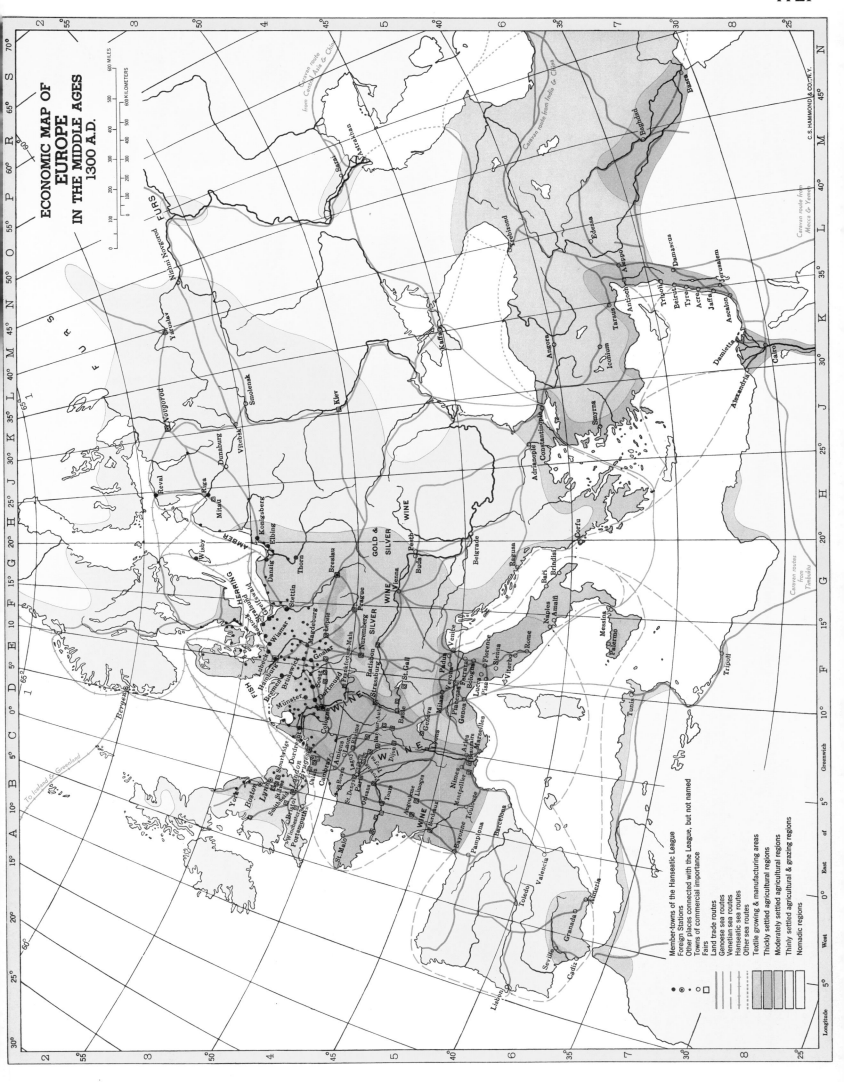

ECONOMIC MAP OF
EUROPE
IN THE MIDDLE AGES
1300 A.D.

C.S. HAMMOND & CO., N.Y.

Member-towns of the Hanseatic League
Foreign Stations
Other places connected with the League, but not named
Towns of commercial importance
Fairs
Land trade routes
Genoese sea routes
Venetian sea routes
Hanseatic sea routes
Other sea routes
Textile growing & manufacturing areas
Thickly settled agricultural regions
Moderately settled agricultural regions
Thinly settled agricultural & grazing regions
Nomadic regions

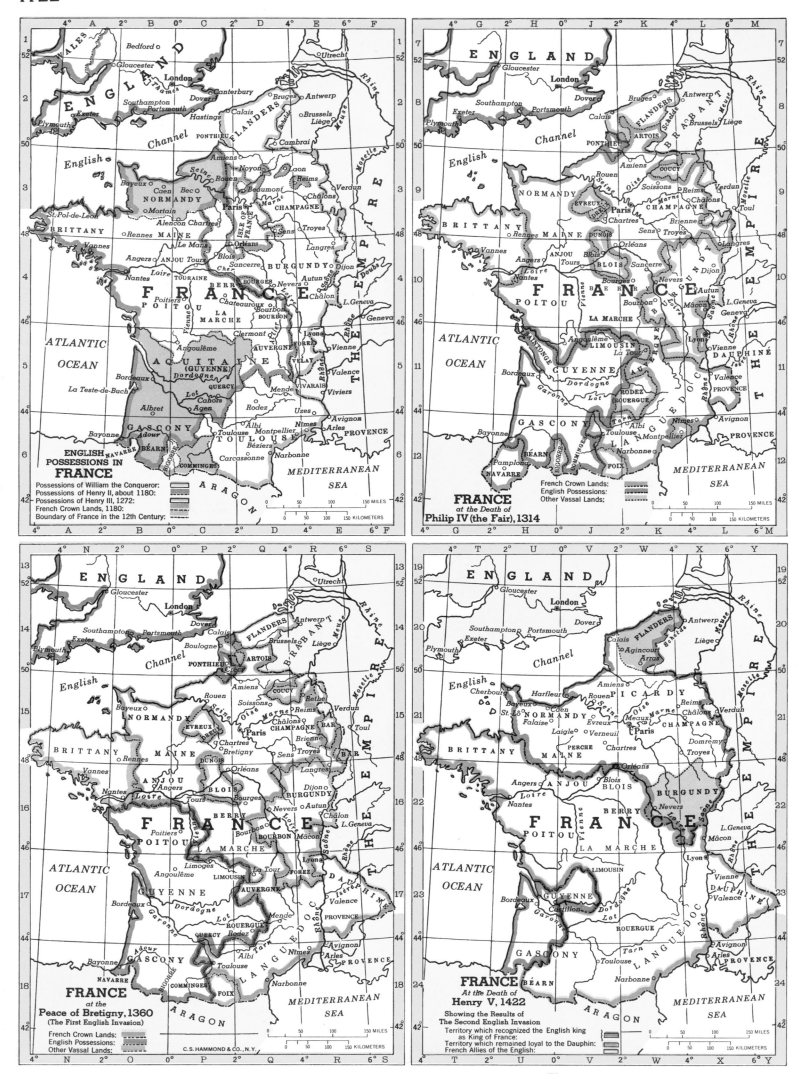

ENGLISH POSSESSIONS IN FRANCE

Possessions of William the Conqueror:
Possessions of Henry II, about 1180:
Possessions of Henry III, 1272:
French Crown Lands, 1180:
Boundary of France in the 12th Century:

FRANCE
at the Death of
Philip IV (the Fair), 1314

French Crown Lands:
English Possessions:
Other Vassal Lands:

FRANCE
at the
Peace of Bretigny, 1360
(The First English Invasion)

French Crown Lands:
English Possessions:
Other Vassal Lands:

C. S. HAMMOND & CO., N.Y.

FRANCE
At the Death of
Henry V, 1422
Showing the Results of
The Second English Invasion
Territory which recognized the English king
as King of France:
Territory which remained loyal to the Dauphin:
French Allies of the English:

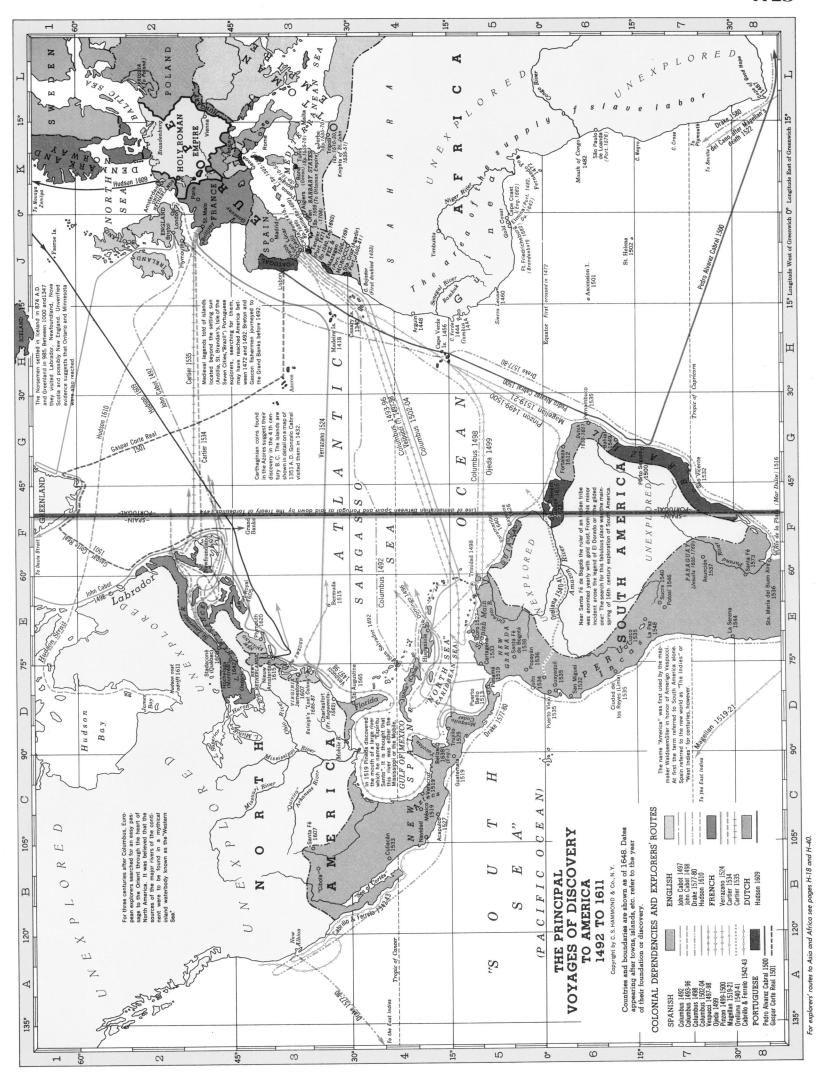

THE PRINCIPAL VOYAGES OF DISCOVERY TO AMERICA 1492 TO 1611

Copyright by C. S. Hammond & Co., N.Y.

Countries and boundaries are shown as of 1648. Dates appearing after towns, islands, etc. refer to the year of their foundation or discovery.

COLONIAL DEPENDENCIES AND EXPLORERS' ROUTES

SPANISH
Columbus 1492
Columbus 1493-96
Columbus 1498
Columbus 1502-04
Vespucci 1497-98
Ojeda 1499
Pinzon 1499-1500
Magellan 1519-21
Orellana 1540-41
Cabrillo & Ferrelo 1542-43

PORTUGUESE
Pedro Alvarez Cabral 1500
Gaspar Corte Real 1501

ENGLISH
John Cabot 1497
John Cabot 1498
Drake 1577-80
Hudson 1610

FRENCH
Verrazano 1524
Cartier 1534
Cartier 1535

DUTCH
Hudson 1609

The name "America" was first used by the map-maker Waldseemüller in honor of Amerigo Vespucci. At first the term referred to South America alone. Spain referred to the new world as "The Indies," or "West Indies" for centuries, however.

The Norsemen settled in Iceland in 874 A.D. and Greenland in 985. Between 1000 and 1347 they visited Labrador, Newfoundland, Nova Scotia and possibly New England. Unverified evidence suggests that Ontario and Minnesota were also reached.

Medieval legends told of islands located beyond the setting sun (Antilia, St. Brandan's, Isle of the Seven Cities, "Brazil"). Portuguese explorers, searching for them, may have reached America between 1472 and 1492. Breton and Gascon fishermen journeyed to the Grand Banks before 1492.

Carthaginian coins found in the Azores suggest their discovery in the 4th century B.C. The islands are shown in detail on a map of 1351 A.D. Gonzalo Cabral visited them in 1432.

For three centuries after Columbus, European explorers searched for an easy passage to the Orient through the heart of North America. It was believed that the sources of the major rivers of the continent were to be found in a mythical inland waterbody known as the "Western Sea."

In 1519 Pineda discovered the mouth of a large river which he named "Espíritu Santo." It is thought that this river was either the Mississippi or the Mobile.

Near Santa Fé de Bogotá the ruler of an Indian tribe was anointed yearly with gold dust. From this minor incident arose the legend of El Dorado or the gilded one. The search for this fabulous place was the main-spring of 16th century exploration of South America.

For explorers' routes to Asia and Africa see pages H-18 and H-40.

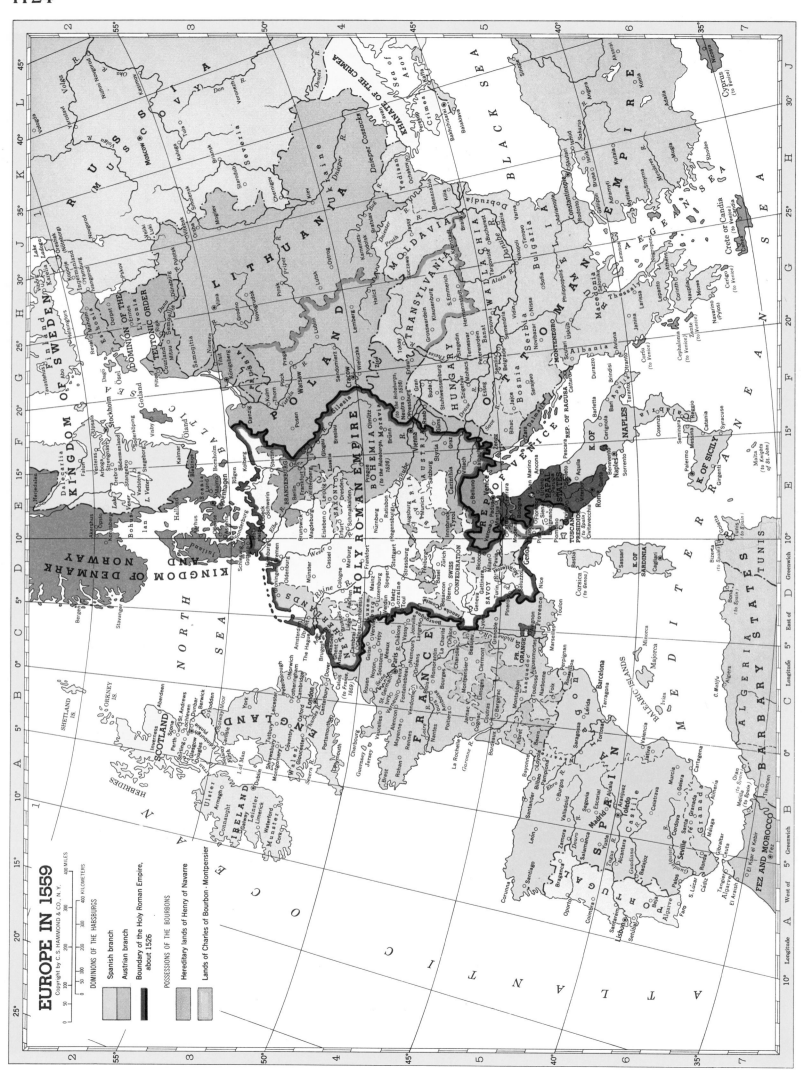

EUROPE IN 1559

Copyright by C. S. HAMMOND & CO., N.Y.

DOMINIONS OF THE HABSBURGS

Spanish branch

Austrian branch

Boundary of the Holy Roman Empire, about 1526

POSSESSIONS OF THE BOURBONS

Hereditary lands of Henry of Navarre

Lands of Charles of Bourbon - Montpensier

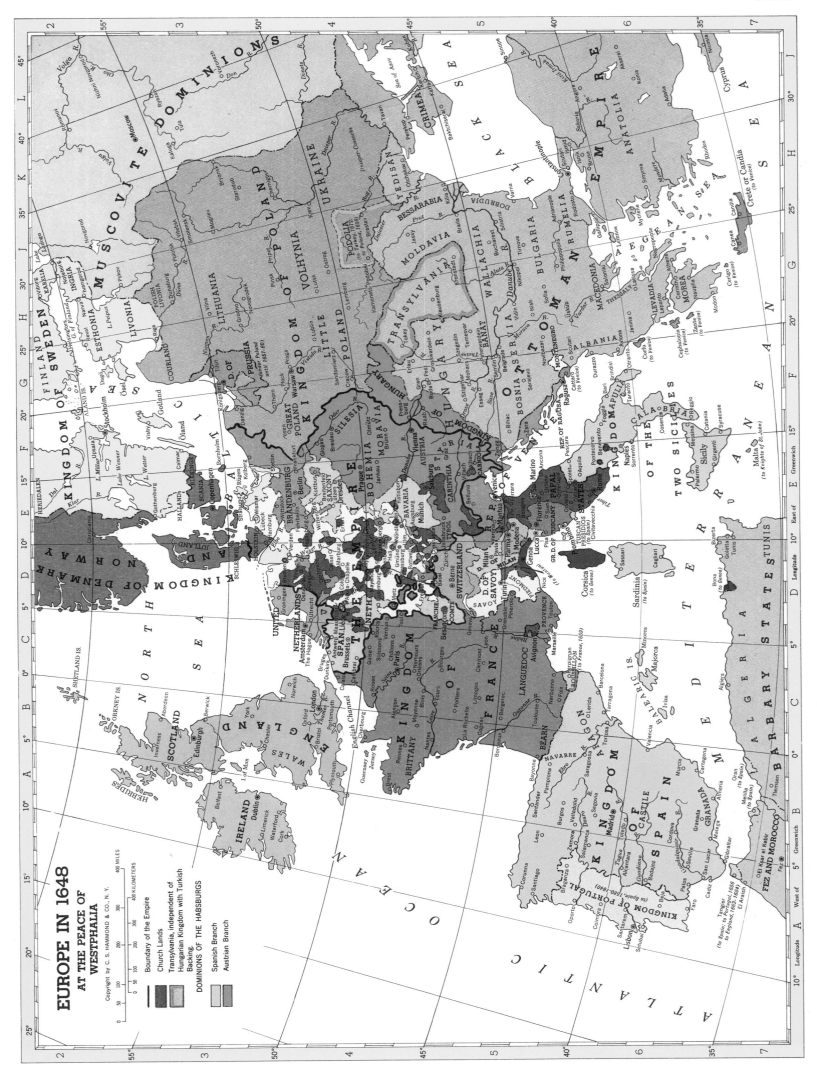

EUROPE IN 1648
AT THE PEACE OF WESTPHALIA

Copyright by C. S. HAMMOND & CO., N.Y.

400 MILES

400 KILOMETERS

— Boundary of the Empire

Church Lands

Transylvania, independent of
Hungarian Kingdom with Turkish
Backing.

DOMINIONS OF THE HABSBURGS

Spanish Branch

Austrian Branch

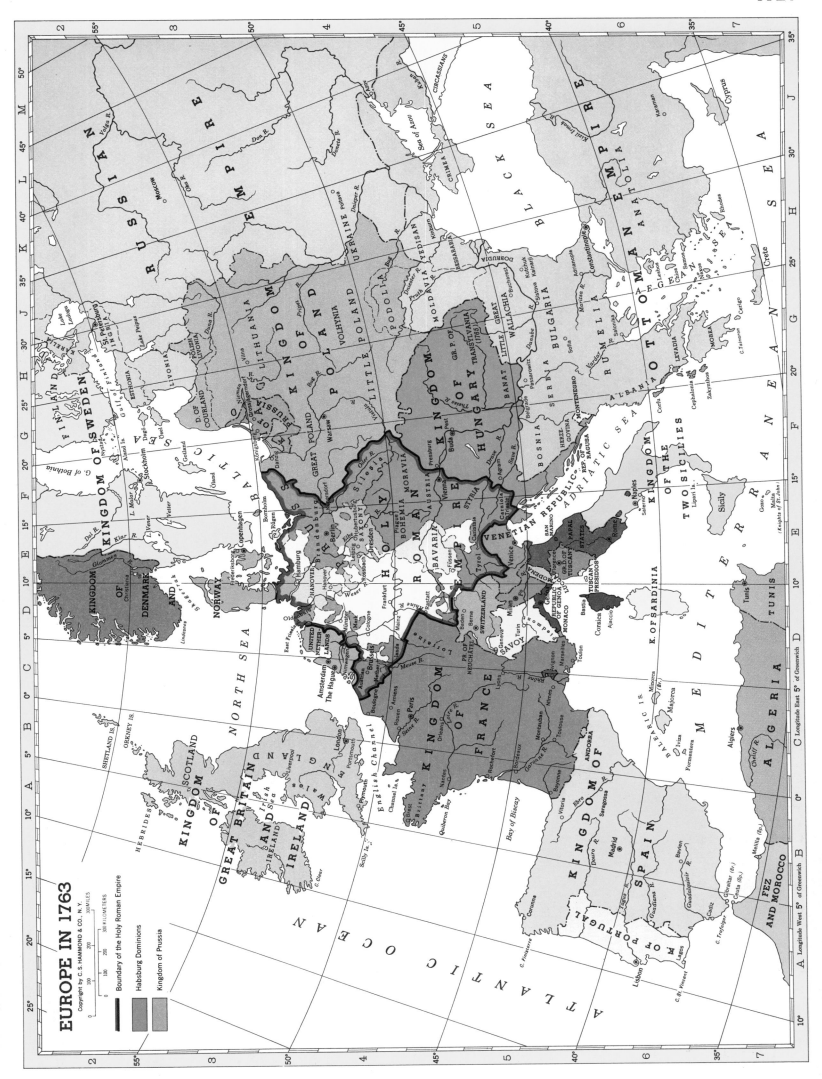

EUROPE IN 1763

Copyright by C.S. HAMMOND & CO., N.Y.

Boundary of the Holy Roman Empire

Habsburg Dominions

Kingdom of Prussia

300 MILES
300 KILOMETERS
0   100   200   300

RUSSIAN EMPIRE

KINGDOM OF SWEDEN

KINGDOM OF DENMARK AND NORWAY

KINGDOM OF GREAT BRITAIN AND IRELAND

KINGDOM OF POLAND

GRAND DUCHY OF LITHUANIA

KINGDOM OF PRUSSIA

HOLY ROMAN EMPIRE

KINGDOM OF HUNGARY

OTTOMAN EMPIRE

KINGDOM OF FRANCE

KINGDOM OF SPAIN

KINGDOM OF PORTUGAL

FEZ AND MOROCCO

ALGERIA

TUNIS

VENETIAN REPUBLIC

PAPAL STATES

KINGDOM OF THE TWO SICILIES

K. OF SARDINIA

ATLANTIC OCEAN

NORTH SEA

MEDITERRANEAN SEA

BLACK SEA

BALTIC SEA

ADRIATIC SEA

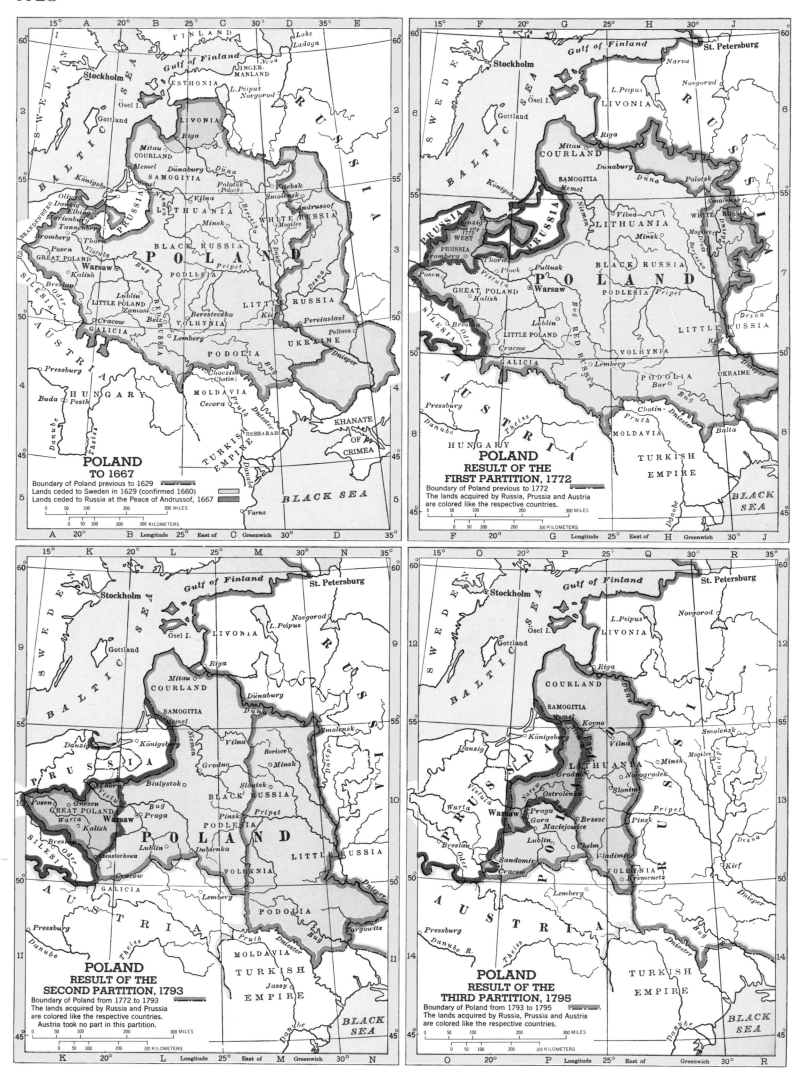

POLAND
TO 1667
Boundary of Poland previous to 1629
Lands ceded to Sweden in 1629 (confirmed 1660)
Lands ceded to Russia at the Peace of Andrussof, 1667

POLAND
RESULT OF THE FIRST PARTITION, 1772
Boundary of Poland previous to 1772
The lands acquired by Russia, Prussia and Austria are colored like the respective countries.

POLAND
RESULT OF THE SECOND PARTITION, 1793
Boundary of Poland from 1772 to 1793
The lands acquired by Russia and Prussia are colored like the respective countries.
Austria took no part in this partition.

POLAND
RESULT OF THE THIRD PARTITION, 1795
Boundary of Poland from 1793 to 1795
The lands acquired by Russia, Prussia and Austria are colored like the respective countries.

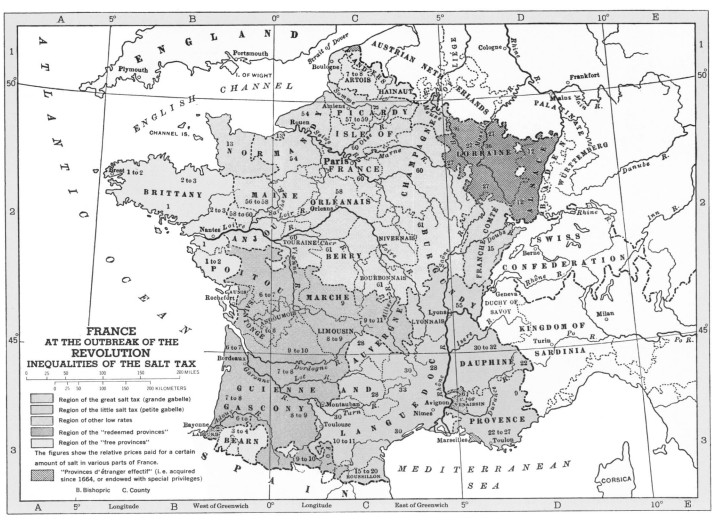

FRANCE
AT THE OUTBREAK OF THE
REVOLUTION
INEQUALITIES OF THE SALT TAX

0 25 50 75 100 150 200 MILES

0 25 50 100 150 200 KILOMETERS

Region of the great salt tax (grande gabelle)

Region of the little salt tax (petite gabelle)

Region of other low rates

Region of the "redeemed provinces"

Region of the "free provinces"

The figures show the relative prices paid for a certain amount of salt in various parts of France.

"Provinces d'étranger effectif" (i.e. acquired since 1664, or endowed with special privileges)

B. Bishopric   C. County

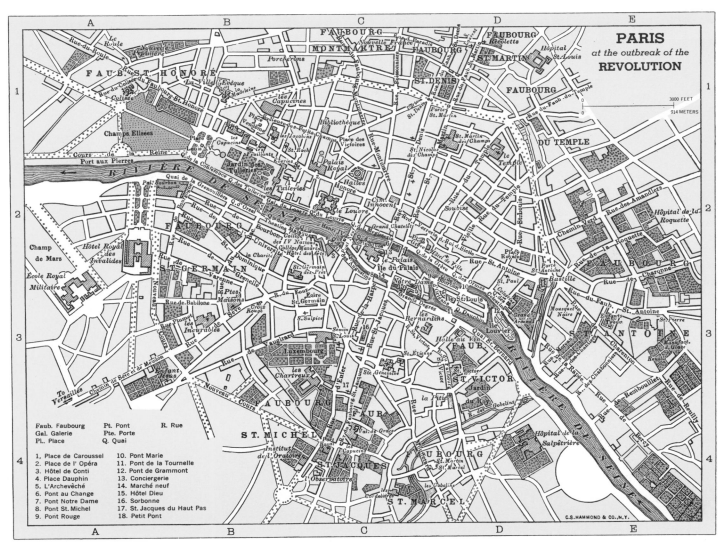

PARIS
at the outbreak of the
REVOLUTION

3000 FEET

914 METERS

Faub. Faubourg   Pt. Pont   R. Rue
Gal. Galerie   Pte. Porte
Pl. Place   Q. Quai

1. Place de Caroussel   10. Pont Marie
2. Place de l' Opéra   11. Pont de la Tournelle
3. Hôtel de Conti   12. Pont de Grammont
4. Place Dauphin   13. Conciergerie
5. L'Archevêché   14. Marché neuf
6. Pont au Change   15. Hôtel Dieu
7. Pont Notre Dame   16. Sorbonne
8. Pont St. Michel   17. St. Jacques du Haut Pas
9. Pont Rouge   18. Petit Pont

C. S. HAMMOND & CO., N.Y.

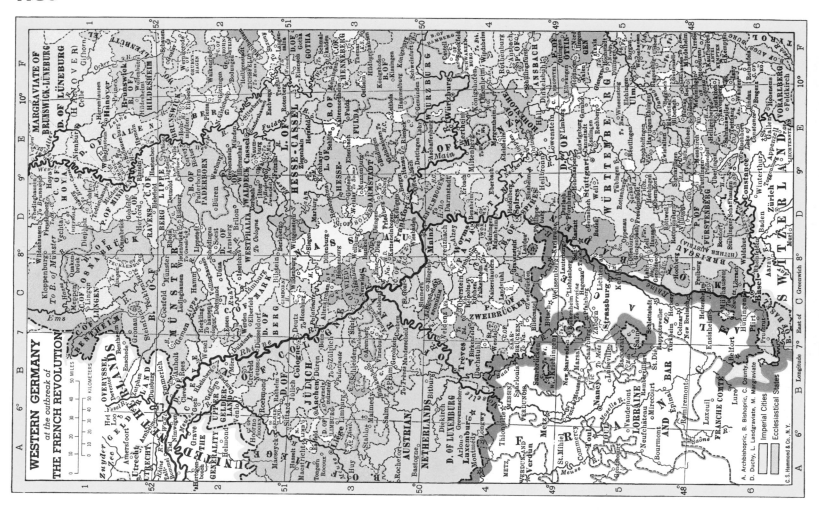

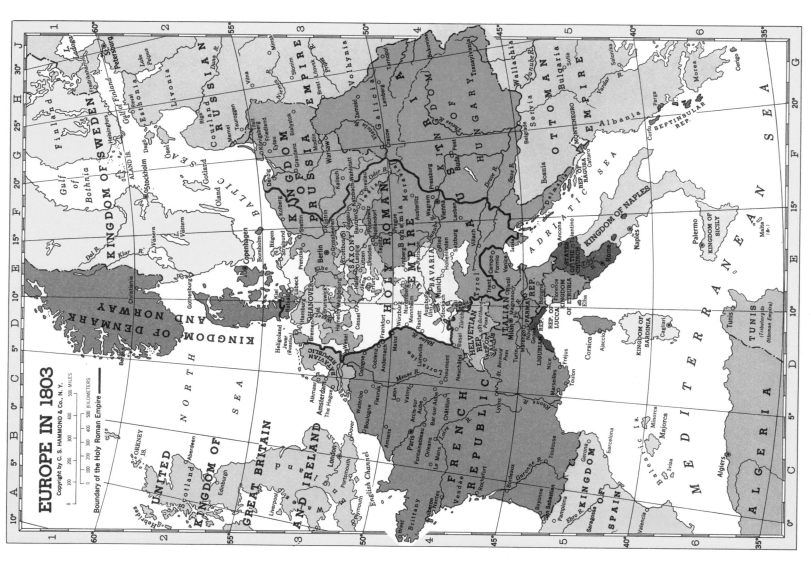

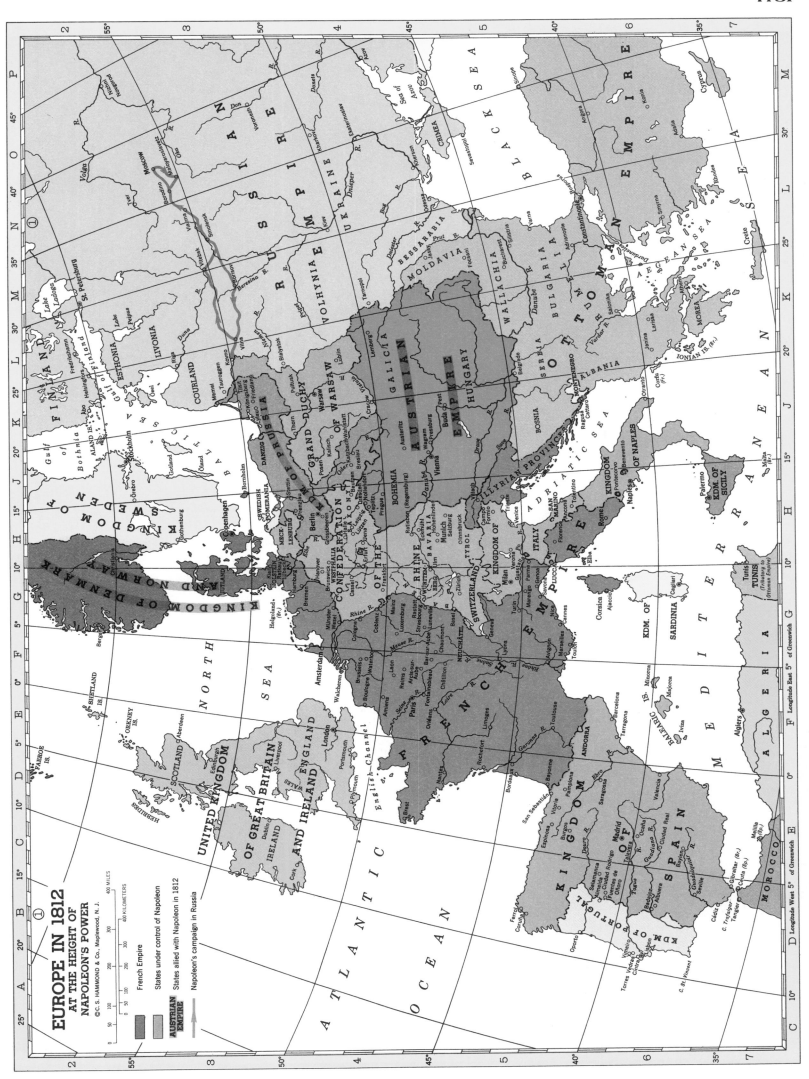

EUROPE IN 1812
AT THE HEIGHT OF NAPOLEON'S POWER

© C. S. HAMMOND & Co., Maplewood, N. J.

French Empire

States under control of Napoleon

States allied with Napoleon in 1812

Napoleon's campaign in Russia

AUSTRIAN EMPIRE

400 MILES

400 KILOMETERS

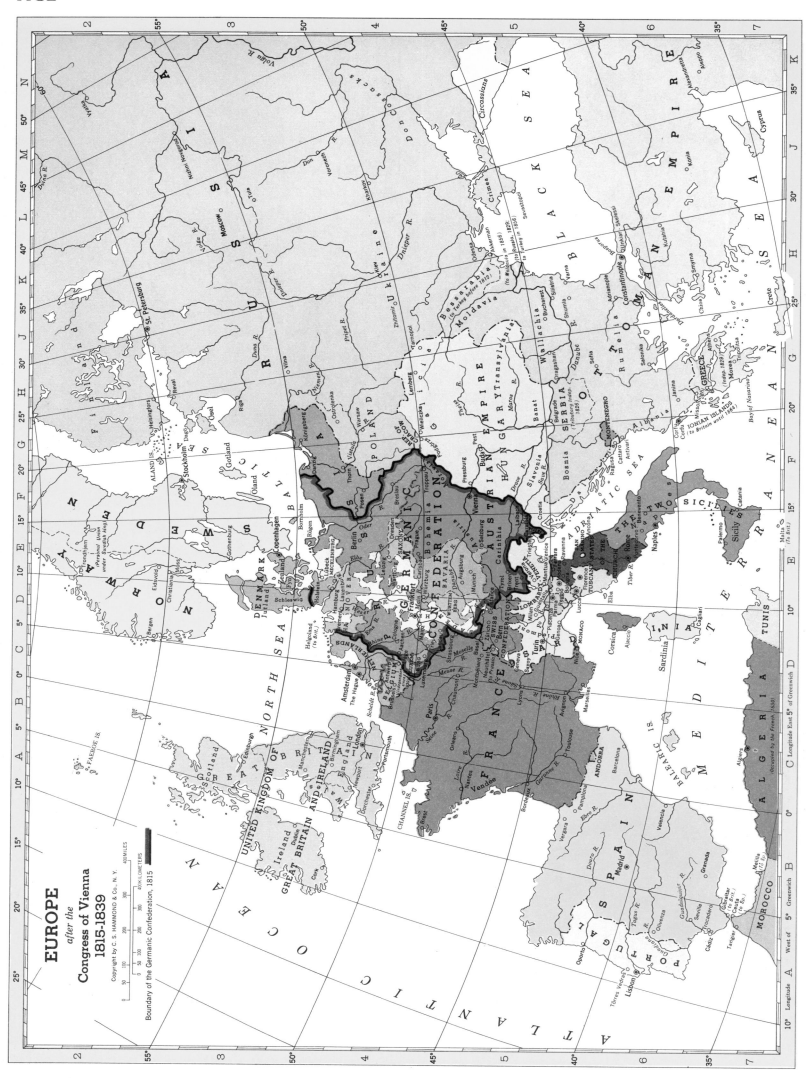

EUROPE
after the
Congress of Vienna
1815-1839

Copyright by C. S. HAMMOND & Co., N.Y.

Boundary of the Germanic Confederation, 1815

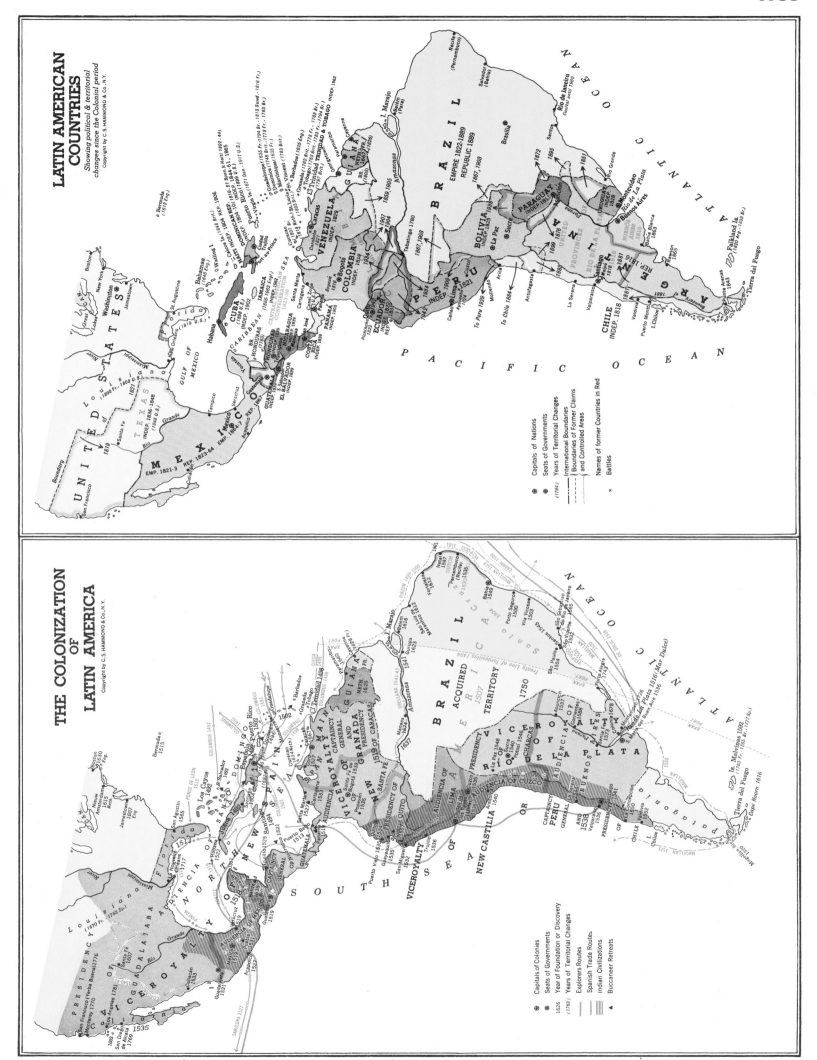

LATIN AMERICAN COUNTRIES

Showing political & territorial
changes since the Colonial period

Copyright by C.S. HAMMOND & Co., N.Y.

THE COLONIZATION OF LATIN AMERICA

Copyright by C.S. HAMMOND & Co., N.Y.

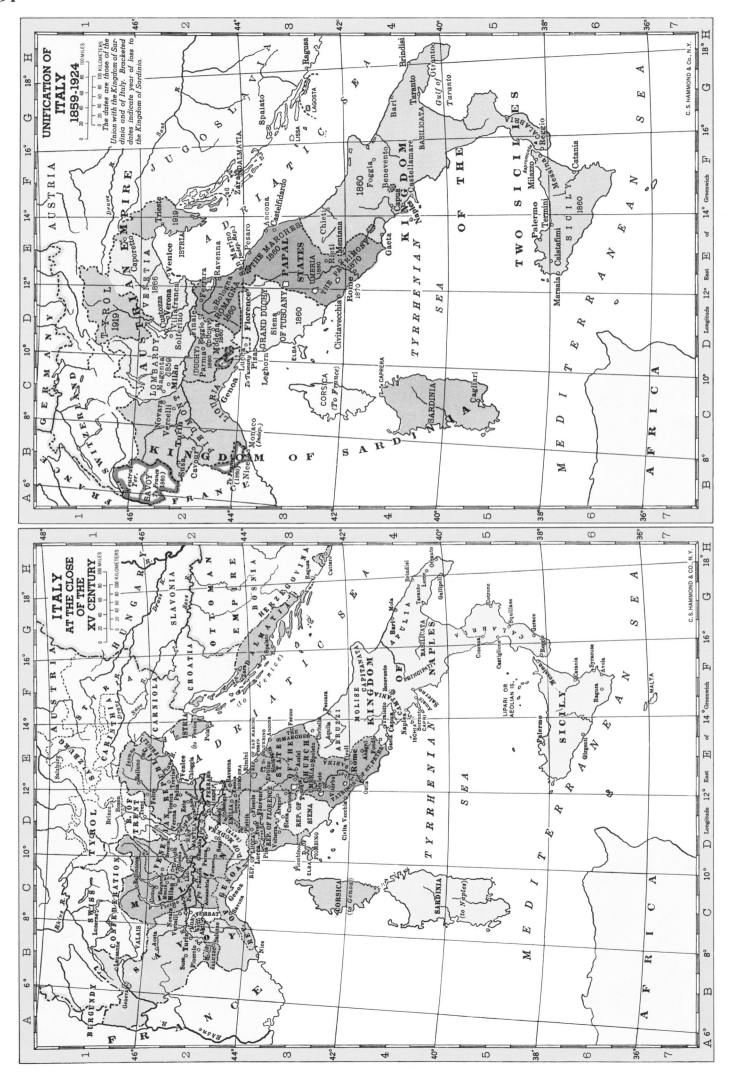

UNIFICATION OF ITALY 1859-1924

The dates are those of the Union with the Kingdom of Sardinia and of Italy. Bracketed dates indicate year of loss to the Kingdom of Sardinia.

ITALY AT THE CLOSE OF THE XV CENTURY

CENTRAL EUROPE
1815-1871

Boundary of German Confederation 1815-1866
Boundary of North German Confederation 1860-1871
Boundary of German Empire in 1871

PEOPLES OF
EUROPE
1910

Copyright by C.S. HAMMOND & Co., N.Y.

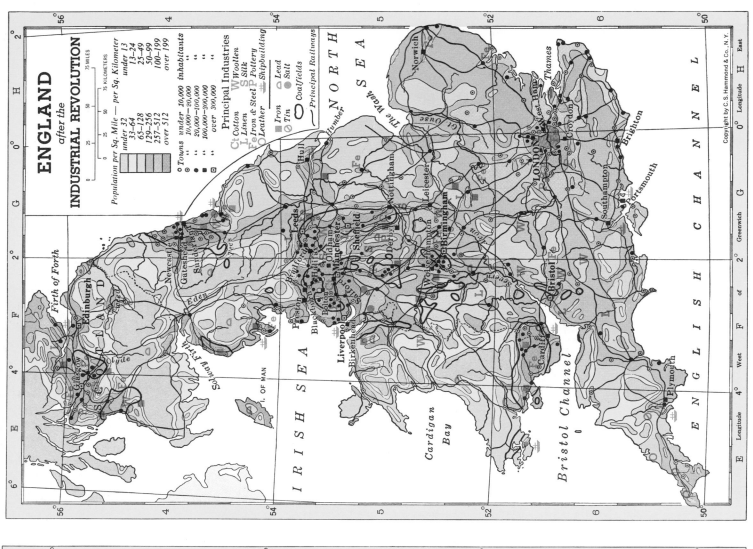

ENGLAND
after the
INDUSTRIAL REVOLUTION

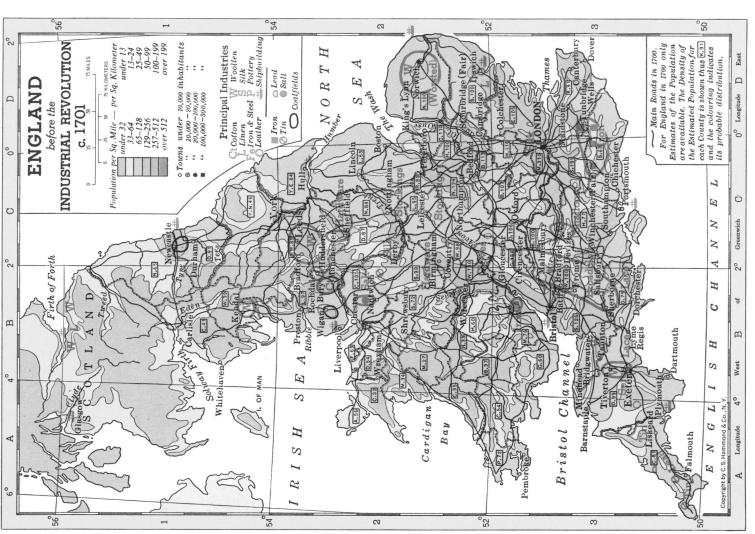

ENGLAND
before the
INDUSTRIAL REVOLUTION
c. 1701

— Main Roads in 1700.
For England in 1700 only
Estimates of the Population
are available. The Density of
the Estimated Population, for
each County is shown thus [K.91]
and the colouring indicates
its probable distribution.

Copyright by C. S. Hammond & Co., N. Y.

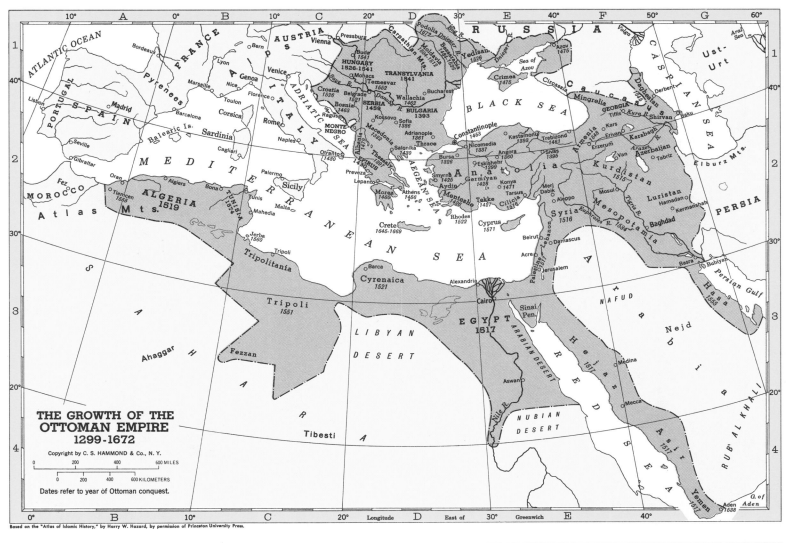

THE GROWTH OF THE OTTOMAN EMPIRE
1299-1672

Copyright by C. S. HAMMOND & Co., N.Y.

Dates refer to year of Ottoman conquest.

Based on the "Atlas of Islamic History," by Harry W. Hazard, by permission of Princeton University Press.

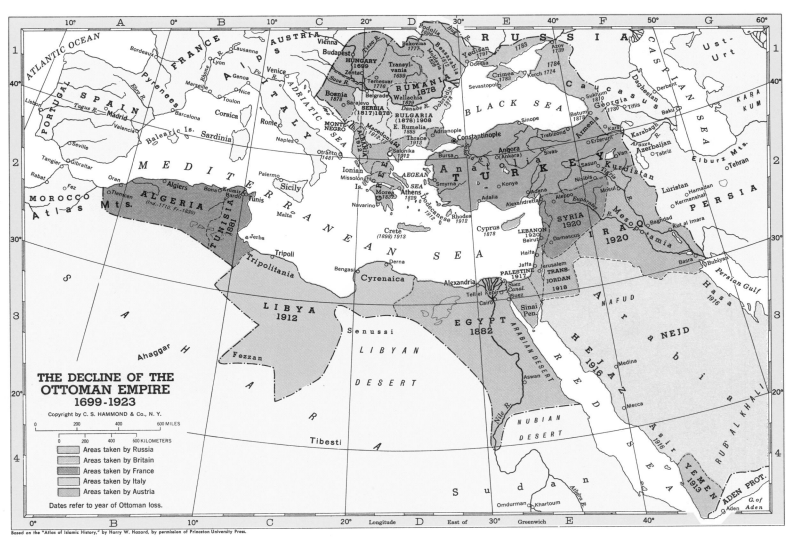

THE DECLINE OF THE OTTOMAN EMPIRE
1699-1923

Copyright by C. S. HAMMOND & Co., N.Y.

- Areas taken by Russia
- Areas taken by Britain
- Areas taken by France
- Areas taken by Italy
- Areas taken by Austria

Dates refer to year of Ottoman loss.

Based on the "Atlas of Islamic History," by Harry W. Hazard, by permission of Princeton University Press.

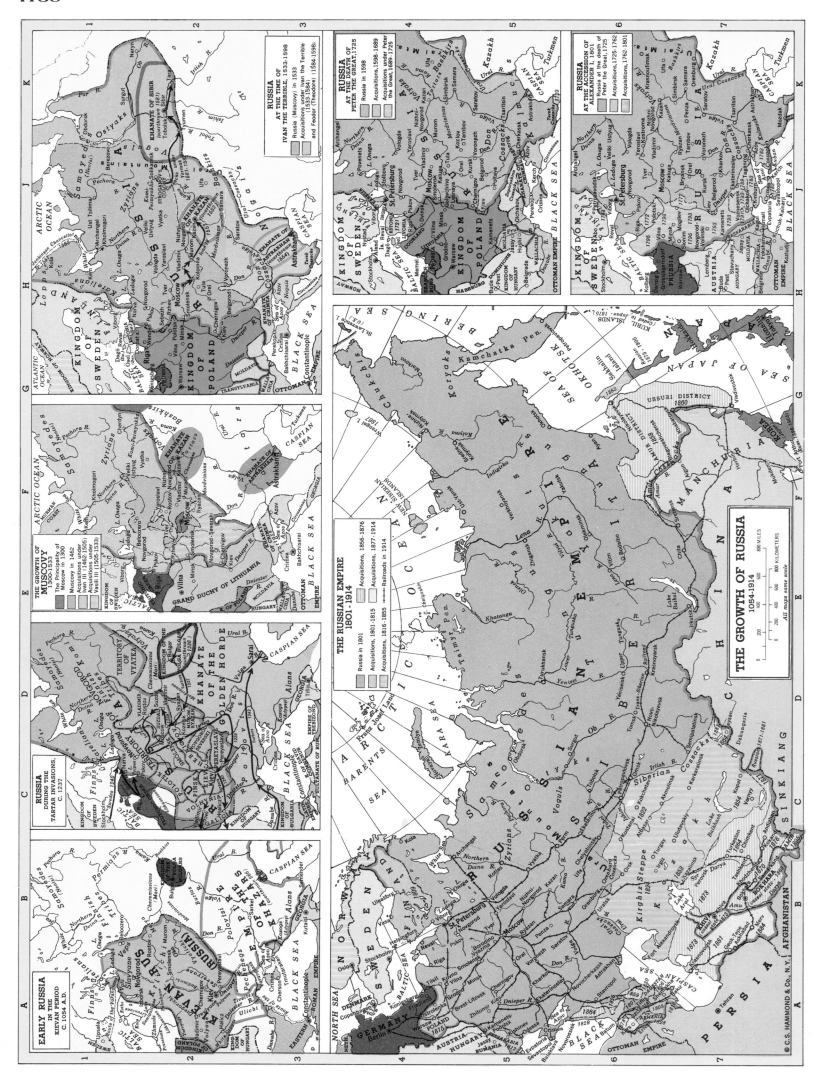

EARLY RUSSIA IN THE KIEVAN PERIOD C. 1054 A.D.

RUSSIA DURING THE TARTAR INVASIONS, C. 1237

THE GROWTH OF MUSCOVY 1300-1533
The Principality of Moscow in 1300
Acquisitions under Ivan III (1462-1505)
Acquisitions under Vasili III (1505-1533)

RUSSIA AT THE TIME OF IVAN THE TERRIBLE, 1533-1598
Russia (Muscovy) in 1533
Acquisitions under Ivan the Terrible (1533-1584)
Acquisitions under Ivan IV and Feodor (Theodore) (1584-1598)

RUSSIA AT THE DEATH OF PETER THE GREAT, 1725
Russia in 1598
Acquisitions, 1598-1689
Acquisitions under Peter the Great, 1689-1725

RUSSIA AT THE ACCESSION OF ALEXANDER I, 1801
Russia at the death of Peter the Great, 1725
Acquisitions, 1725-1762
Acquisitions, 1762-1801

THE RUSSIAN EMPIRE 1801-1914
Russia in 1801
Acquisitions, 1801-1815
Acquisitions, 1816-1855
Acquisitions, 1856-1876
Acquisitions, 1877-1914
Railroads in 1914

THE GROWTH OF RUSSIA 1054-1914

MILES
0 200 400 600 800
0 200 400 600 800 KILOMETERS
All maps same scale

© C.S. Hammond & Co., N.Y.

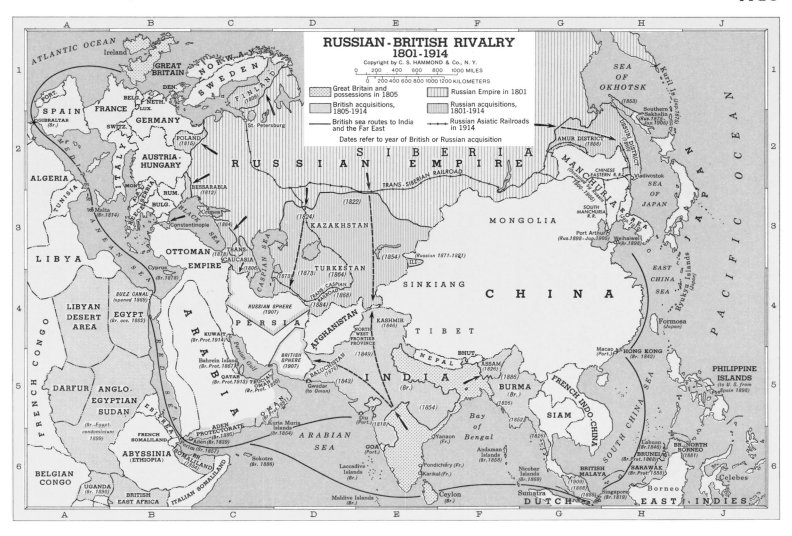

RUSSIAN-BRITISH RIVALRY
1801-1914

Copyright by C. S. HAMMOND & Co., N. Y.

0   200   400   600   800   1000 MILES
0   200 400 600 800 1000 1200 KILOMETERS

Great Britain and possessions in 1805

British acquisitions, 1805-1914

Russian Empire in 1801

Russian acquisitions, 1801-1914

British sea routes to India and the Far East

Russian Asiatic Railroads in 1914

Dates refer to year of British or Russian acquisition

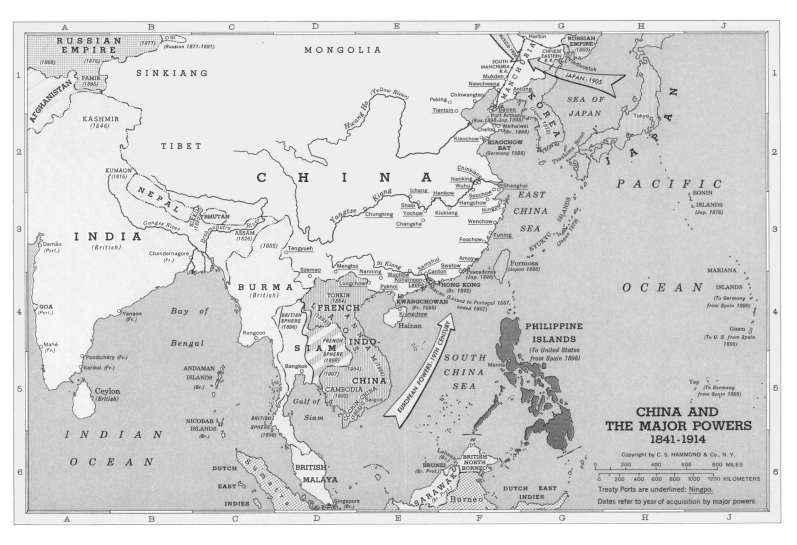

CHINA AND
THE MAJOR POWERS
1841-1914

Copyright by C. S. HAMMOND & Co., N. Y.

0   200   400   600   800 MILES
0   200 400 600 800 1000 1200 KILOMETERS

Treaty Ports are underlined: Ningpo.

Dates refer to year of acquisition by major powers.

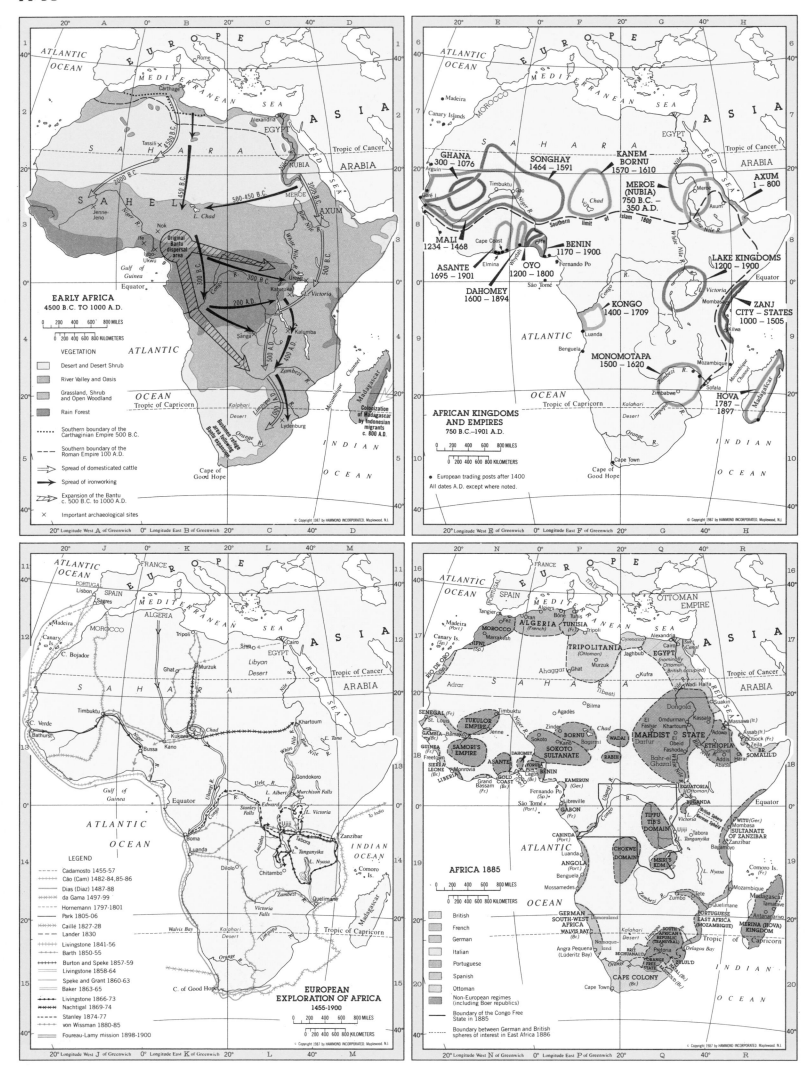

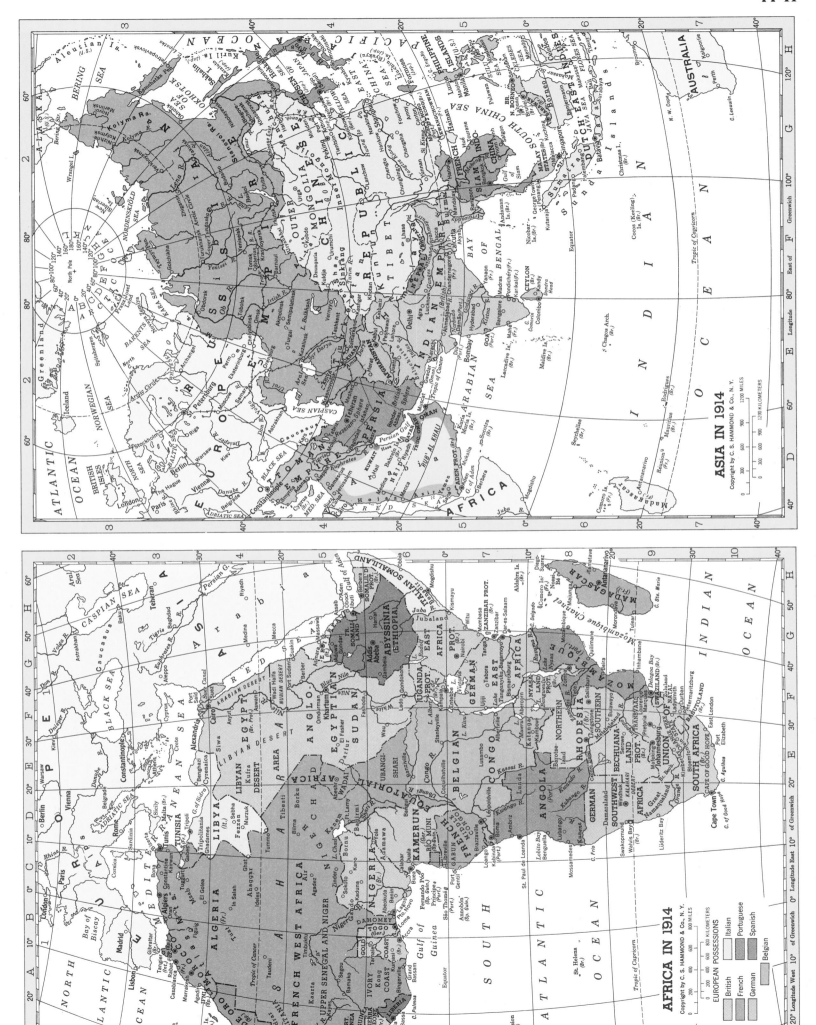

ASIA IN 1914

Copyright by C. S. HAMMOND & Co., N. Y.

AFRICA IN 1914

Copyright by C. S. HAMMOND & Co., N. Y.

EUROPEAN POSSESSIONS

British | Italian
French | Portuguese
German | Spanish
Belgian

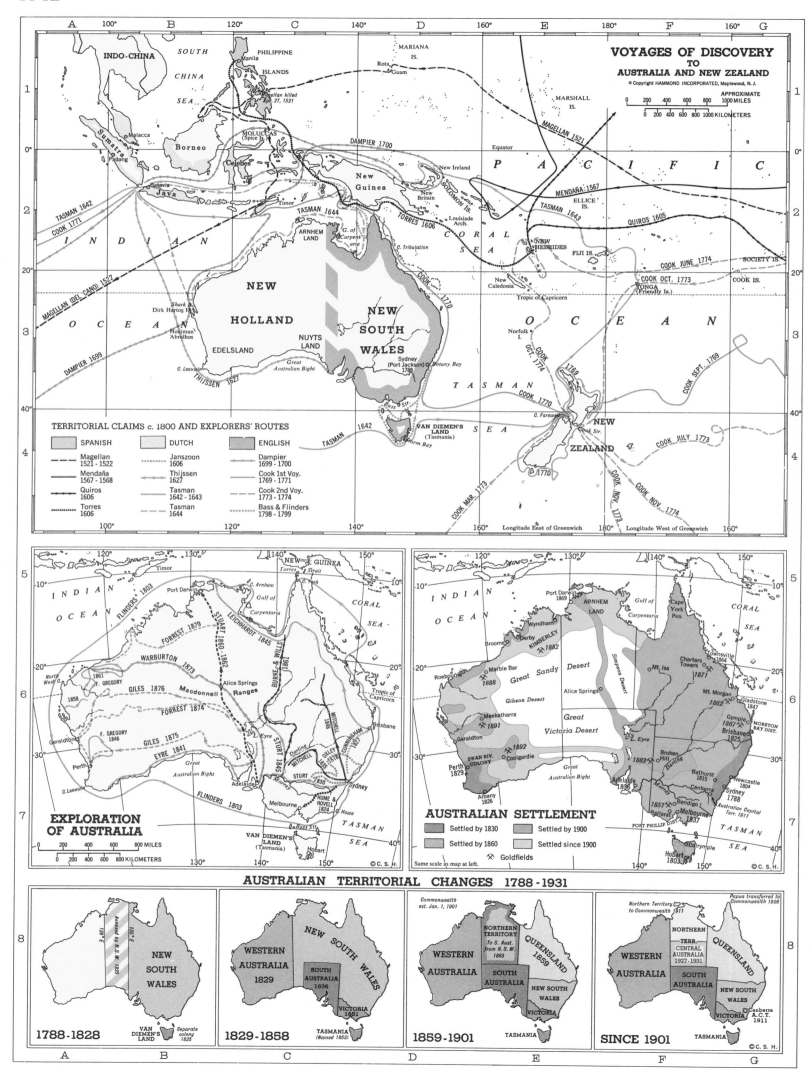

VOYAGES OF DISCOVERY
TO
AUSTRALIA AND NEW ZEALAND
© Copyright HAMMOND INCORPORATED, Maplewood, N. J.

TERRITORIAL CLAIMS c. 1800 AND EXPLORERS' ROUTES

SPANISH   DUTCH   ENGLISH

Magellan 1521 - 1522
Mendaña 1567 - 1568
Quiros 1606
Torres 1606
Janszoon 1606
Thijssen 1627
Tasman 1642 - 1643
Tasman 1644
Dampier 1699 - 1700
Cook 1st Voy. 1769 - 1771
Cook 2nd Voy. 1773 - 1774
Bass & Flinders 1798 - 1799

EXPLORATION OF AUSTRALIA

AUSTRALIAN SETTLEMENT

Settled by 1830
Settled by 1860
Settled by 1900
Settled since 1900
Goldfields

AUSTRALIAN TERRITORIAL CHANGES 1788-1931

1788-1828

1829-1858

1859-1901

SINCE 1901

EXPLORATION OF CANADA

© Copyright HAMMOND INCORPORATED, Maplewood, N.J.

0 50 100 200 300 400 MILES

0 50 100 200 300 400 KILOMETERS

Forts & fur traders posts .... Battles ✕✕

The various Indian tribes are shown where they were located during the period of their greatest significance in Canadian history.

THE GROWTH OF CANADA
FROM 1791 TO 1949

Copyright by C.S. HAMMOND & Co., N.Y.

The dates within the provinces, territories or districts indicate the years of their creation as political divisions.

1791

1873

1898

1949

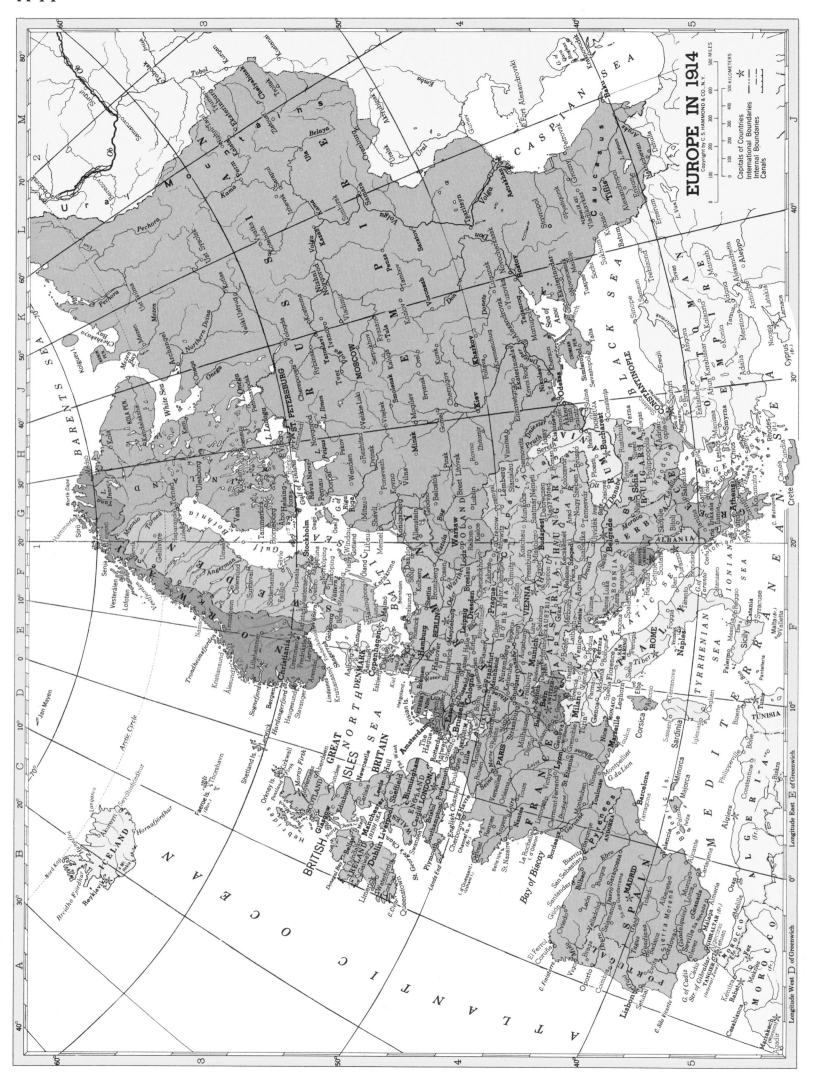

EUROPE IN 1914

Copyright by C. S. HAMMOND & CO., N.Y.

Capitals of Countries ☆
International Boundaries ___
Internal Boundaries ...
Canals

500 KILOMETERS
500 MILES

EUROPE AND THE NEAR EAST

0 100 200 300 400 500 MILES
0 100 200 300 400 500 KILOMETERS

- - - - Stabilized Line on the Western Front, 1914-1917
- - - - Eastern Front on the Eve of the Russian Revolution, Oct. 1917
· · · · · Limit of Allied Advances in the East
Area Occupied by the Central Powers after Brest Litovsk Treaty, 1918

THE FIRST WORLD WAR
1914-1918

© C. S. HAMMOND & Co., Maplewood, N. J.

The Allies
Neutral States
The Central Powers
Areas Occupied by the Central Powers
Advances of the Allies
Advances of the Central Powers

THE WESTERN FRONT

0 20 40 60 80 MILES
0 20 40 60 80 KILOMETERS

──── Limit of German Advance, 1914
──── Limit of Trench Warfare, 1914-1917
- - - - Hindenburg Line, 1917
━━━━ Limit of Final German Advance, 1918
········ Armistice Line, November 11, 1918
━━━━ Limit of Allied Occupation Zone

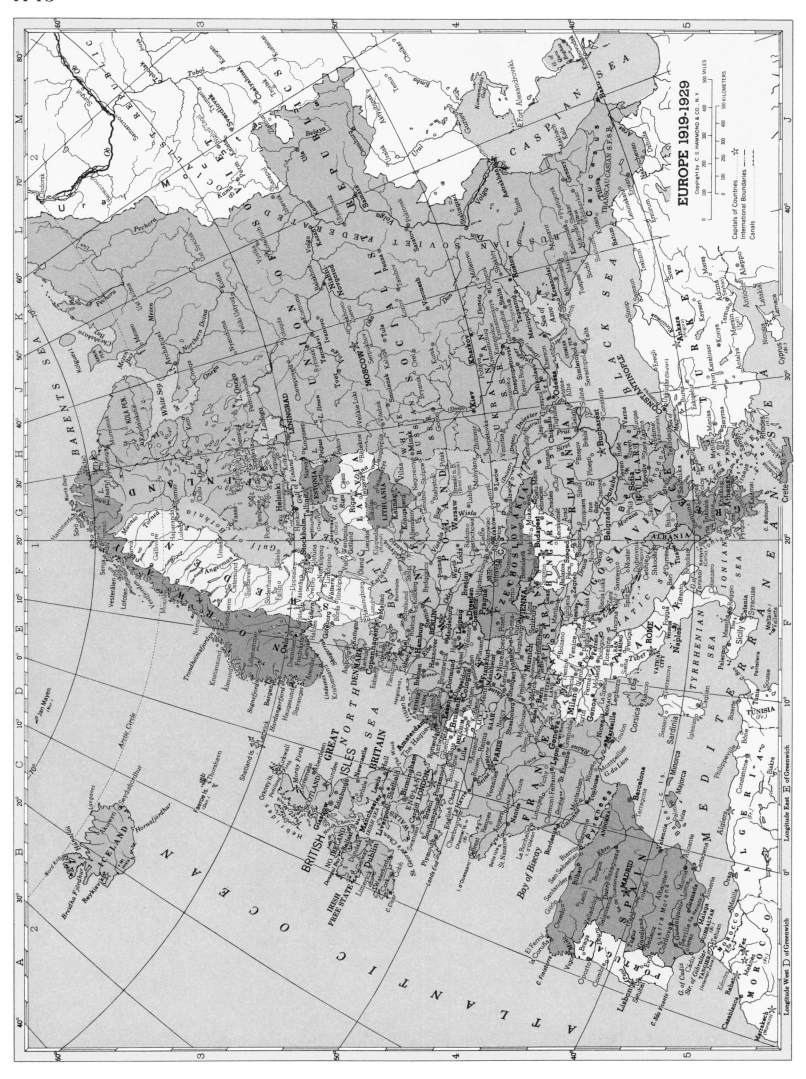

EUROPE 1919-1929

Copyright by C. S. HAMMOND & CO., N.Y.

Capitals of Countries
International Boundaries
Canals

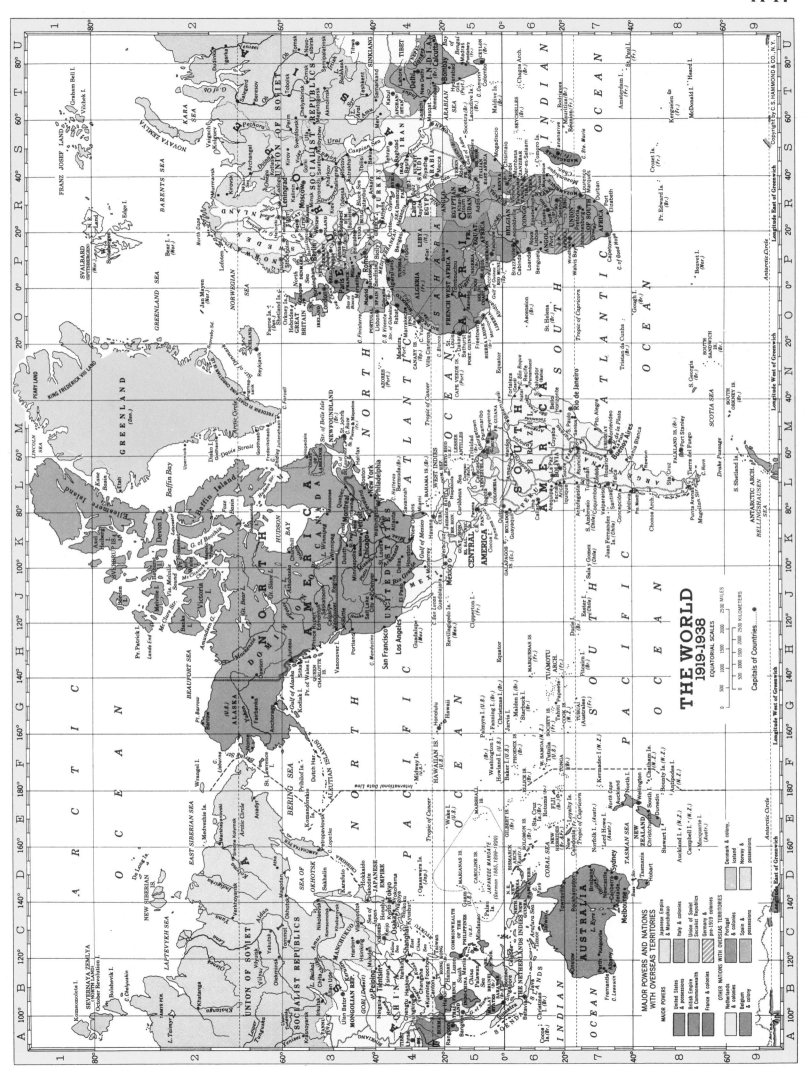

THE WORLD
1919-1938

EQUATORIAL SCALES

Capitals of Countries..........●

MAJOR POWERS AND NATIONS
WITH OVERSEAS TERRITORIES

MAJOR POWERS
United States
& possessions
British Empire
& Commonwealth
France & colonies

OTHER NATIONS WITH OVERSEAS TERRITORIES
Netherlands
& colonies
Belgium
& colony

Japanese Empire
& Manchukuo
Italy & colonies
Union of Soviet
Socialist Republics
Germany &
pre-1919 colonies

Portugal
& colonies
Spain &
possessions

Denmark & colony
Iceland
Norway &
possessions

Copyright by C. S. HAMMOND & CO., N.Y.

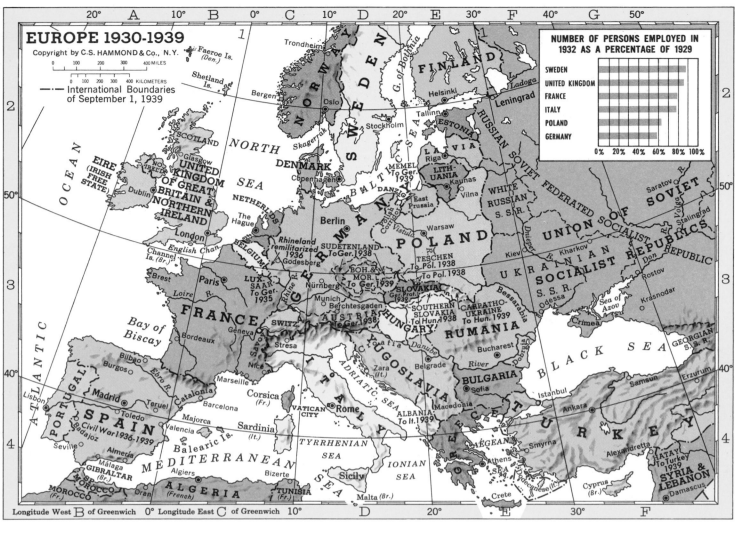

EUROPE 1930-1939

Copyright by C.S. Hammond & Co., N.Y.

0 100 200 300 400 MILES
0 100 200 300 400 KILOMETERS

International Boundaries of September 1, 1939

NUMBER OF PERSONS EMPLOYED IN 1932 AS A PERCENTAGE OF 1929

SWEDEN
UNITED KINGDOM
FRANCE
ITALY
POLAND
GERMANY

0% 20% 40% 60% 80% 100%

ATLANTIC OCEAN

Faeroe Is. (Den.)
Shetland Is.
Trondheim
Bergen
Oslo
NORWAY
SWEDEN
Stockholm
Skagerrak
NORTH SEA
DENMARK
Copenhagen
G. of Bothnia
FINLAND
Helsinki
L. Ladoga
Leningrad
Tallinn
ESTONIA
Riga
LATVIA
BALTIC SEA
MEMEL To Ger. 1939
LITH-UANIA
Kaunas
Vilna
WHITE RUSSIAN S.S.R.
RUSSIAN SOVIET FEDERATED SOCIALIST
Saratov
SOVIET
SOCIALIST
UNION OF
REPUBLICS
Stalingrad
Kharkov
UKRAINIAN S.S.R.
Kiev
Don
Rostov
REPUBLIC
Dnieper
Krasnodar
Sea of Azov
Odessa
Bessarabia
Crimea
GEORGIAN S.S.R.
BLACK SEA
Samsun
Erzurum
T U R K E Y
Ankara
Alexandretta
HATAY To Turkey 1939
SYRIA & LEBANON
Damascus
Cyprus (Br.)

SCOTLAND
Glasgow
EIRE (IRISH FREE STATE)
Dublin
UNITED KINGDOM OF GREAT BRITAIN & NORTHERN IRELAND
NO. IRELAND
London
English Chan.
Channel Is. (Br.)
Brest
NETHERL'DS
The Hague
BELGIUM
Berlin
Rhineland remilitarized 1936 Godesberg
SUDETENLAND To Ger. 1938
POLAND
Warsaw
Vistula
Corridor
DANZIG
East Prussia
TESCHEN To Pol. 1938
To Pol. 1938
BOH. & MOR. To Ger. 1939
SLOVAKIA Prot. 1939
SOUTHERN SLOVAKIA To Hun. 1938
CARPATHO-UKRAINE To Hun. 1939

G E R M A N Y
LUX.
SAAR To Ger. 1935
Nürnberg
Munich
Rhine R.
SWITZ.
Stresa
AUSTRIA To Ger. 1938
Berchtesgaden
HUNGARY
Danube
RUMANIA
Bucharest
Danube River
BULGARIA
Sofia
Macedonia
Istanbul
AEGEAN SEA
Smyrna

F R A N C E
Paris
Loire R.
Bordeaux
Bay of Biscay
Geneva
Nice
Marseille
Savoie
Po R.
YUGOSLAVIA
Zara (It.)
Belgrade
ADRIATIC SEA
Bay of Biscay

PORTUGAL
Lisbon
Madrid
Toledo
Teruel
SPAIN
Civil War 1936-1939
Burgos
Bilbao
Ebro R.
Catalonia
Barcelona
Valencia
Majorca
Sardinia (It.)
Corsica (Fr.)
Balearic Is.
VATICAN CITY
Rome
ITALY
ALBANIA To It. 1939
GREECE
Athens
Crete

Badajoz
Seville
Almería
Málaga
GIBRALTAR (Br.)
Algiers
ALGERIA (French)
MOROCCO (Sp.)
MOROCCO (Fr.)
Oran
MEDITERRANEAN SEA
TUNISIA (Fr.)
Bizerte
Sicily
TYRRHENIAN SEA
IONIAN SEA
Malta (Br.)
Dodecanese (It.)

Longitude West B of Greenwich   0° Longitude East C of Greenwich   10°   D   20°   E   30°   F'

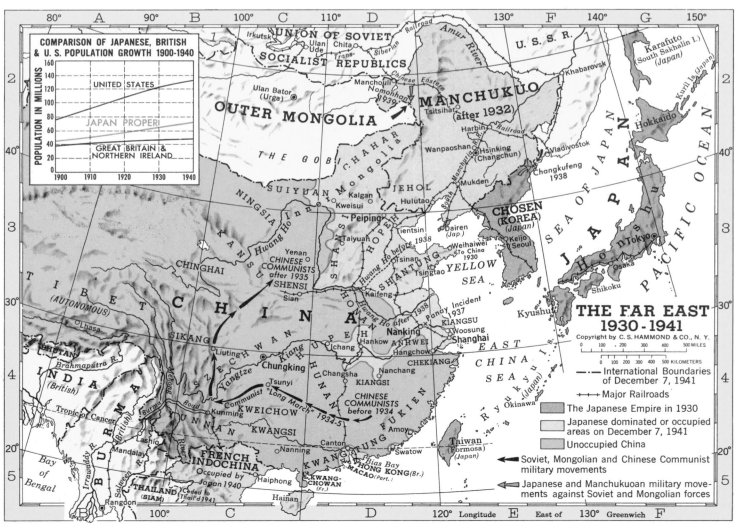

COMPARISON OF JAPANESE, BRITISH & U.S. POPULATION GROWTH 1900-1940

POPULATION IN MILLIONS

160
140
120
100
80
60
40
20

UNITED STATES
JAPAN PROPER
GREAT BRITAIN & NORTHERN IRELAND

1900 1910 1920 1930 1940

Irkutsk
Ulan Ude
Chita
UNION OF SOVIET SOCIALIST REPUBLICS
Trans-Siberian
Railroad
Amur River
U.S.S.R.
Chinese Eastern Railroad
Khabarovsk
Karafuto (South Sakhalin I.) (Japan)

Ulan Bator (Urga)
OUTER MONGOLIA
Manchouli
Nomonhan 1939
MANCHUKUO (after 1932)
Tsitsihar
Harbin
Railroad
Vladivostok
Changkufeng 1938
Kuril Is. (Japan)

THE GOBI
Inner Mongolia
CHAHAR
Wanpaoshan
Manchuria
Hsinking (Changchun)
Mukden
Chinese Eastern
Hokkaido

NINGSIA
SUIYUAN
Kalgan
Kweisui
JEHOL
Hulutao
SEA OF JAPAN
PACIFIC OCEAN

KANSU
Peiping
HOPEI
Tientsin
Dairen (Jap.)
Weihaiwei To China 1930
CHOSEN (KOREA) (Japan)
Keijo (Seoul)
J A P A N
Tokyo
Honshu

CHINGHAI
Yenan
CHINESE COMMUNISTS after 1935
SHENSI
Sian
SHANSI
Taiyuan
Hwang Ho before 1938
Tsinan
SHANTUNG
Tsingtao
YELLOW SEA
Osaka
Shikoku

TIBET (AUTONOMOUS)
Lhasa
C H I N A
SIKANG
Liuting
SZECHWAN
Chungking
Tsunyi
"Long March" 1934-5
KWEICHOW
Kunming
YUNNAN
Hwang Ho after 1938
HONAN
Kaifeng
HUPEH
Hankow
Ichang
Hangchow
ANHWEI
Nanking
Woosung
Shanghai
CHEKIANG
Panay Incident 1937
KIANGSU
EAST CHINA SEA
Kyushu
Ryukyu Is. (Japan)
Okinawa

THE FAR EAST 1930-1941

Copyright by C.S. Hammond & Co., N.Y.

0 100 200 300 400 500 MILES
0 100 200 300 400 500 KILOMETERS

International Boundaries of December 7, 1941
Major Railroads
The Japanese Empire in 1930
Japanese dominated or occupied areas on December 7, 1941
Unoccupied China
Soviet, Mongolian and Chinese Communist military movements
Japanese and Manchukuoan military movements against Soviet and Mongolian forces

INDIA (British)
Brahmaputra R.
BHUTAN
Tropic of Cancer
BURMA (British)
Lashio
Mandalay
Irrawaddy R.
Salween R.
Mekong R.
Bay of Bengal
Rangoon
FRENCH INDOCHINA
Occupied by Japan 1940
THAILAND (SIAM)
Haiphong
Hainan

Changsha
HUNAN
KIANGSI
Nanchang
FUKIEN
Amoy
Canton
KWANGTUNG
KWANGSI
Nanning
Swatow
Bias Bay
HONG KONG (Br.)
MACAO (Port.)
KWANGCHOWAN (Fr.)
Ceded to Thail'd 1941
CHINESE COMMUNISTS before 1934
Communist Road "Long March" 1934-5
Taiwan (Formosa) (Japan)

80°   A   90°   B   100°   C   110°   D   120° Longitude E   East of 130° Greenwich   F'
130°   F   140°   G   150°

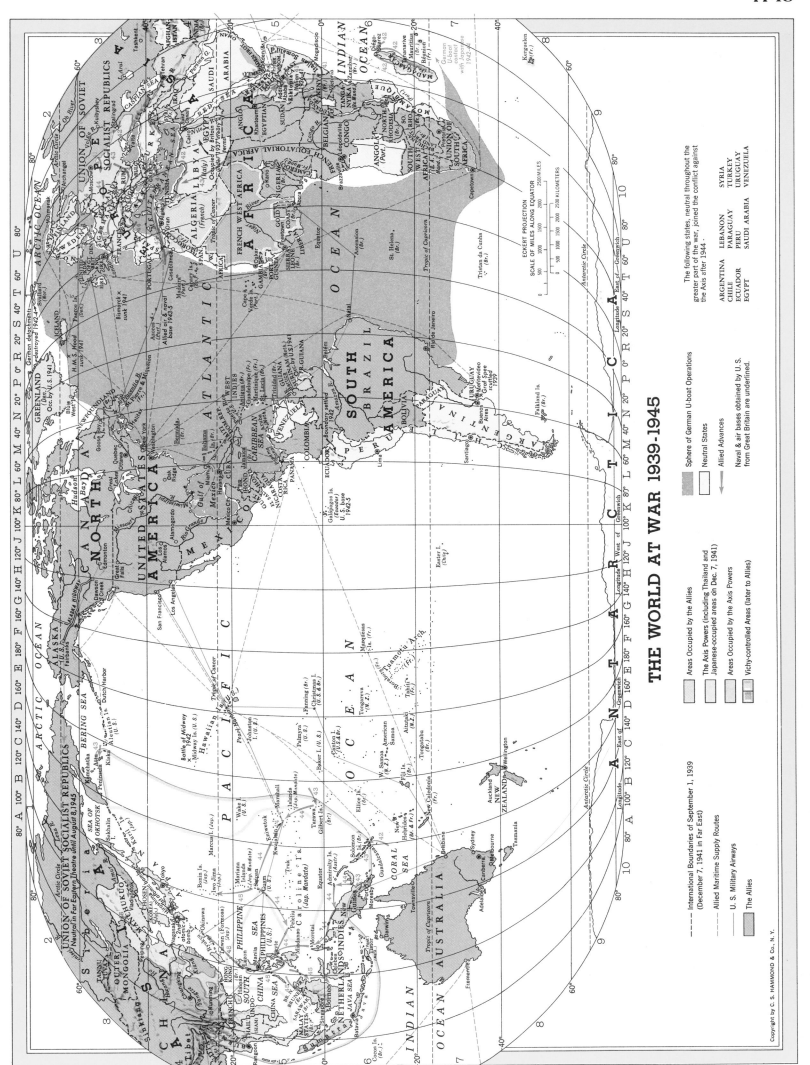

THE WORLD AT WAR 1939-1945

The following states, neutral throughout the greater part of the war, joined the conflict against the Axis after 1944 .

ARGENTINA	LEBANON	SYRIA
CHILE	PARAGUAY	TURKEY
ECUADOR	PERU	URUGUAY
EGYPT	SAUDI ARABIA	VENEZUELA

Sphere of German U-boat Operations

Neutral States

Allied Advances

Naval & air bases obtained by U.S. from Great Britain are underlined.

International Boundaries of September 1, 1939 (December 7, 1941 in Far East)

Allied Maritime Supply Routes

U. S. Military Airways

The Allies

Areas Occupied by the Allies

The Axis Powers (including Thailand and Japanese-occupied areas on Dec. 7, 1941)

Areas Occupied by the Axis Powers

Vichy-controlled Areas (later to Allies)

ECKERT PROJECTION

SCALE OF MILES ALONG EQUATOR

Copyright by C. S. HAMMOND & Co., N.Y.

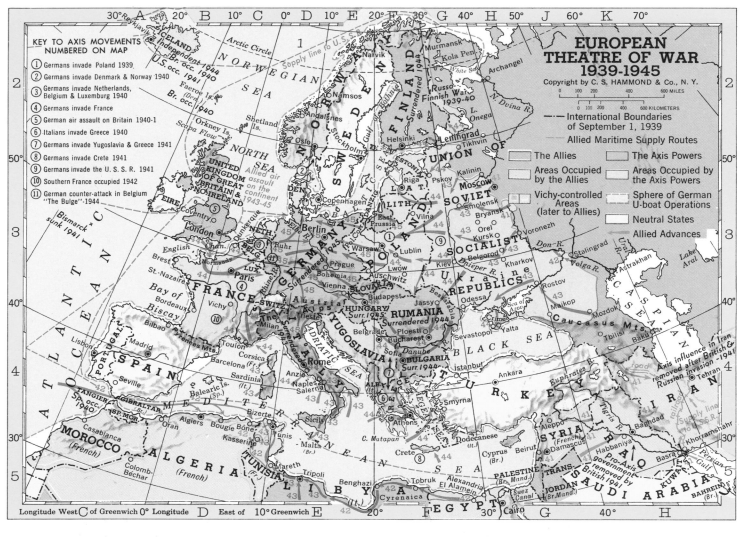

KEY TO AXIS MOVEMENTS NUMBERED ON MAP

① Germans invade Poland 1939
② Germans invade Denmark & Norway 1940
③ Germans invade Netherlands, Belgium & Luxemburg 1940
④ Germans invade France
⑤ German air assault on Britain 1940-1
⑥ Italians invade Greece 1940
⑦ Germans invade Yugoslavia & Greece 1941
⑧ Germans invade Crete 1941
⑨ Germans invade the U.S.S.R. 1941
⑩ Southern France occupied 1942
⑪ German counter-attack in Belgium "The Bulge"-1944

EUROPEAN THEATRE OF WAR 1939-1945
Copyright by C. S. HAMMOND & Co., N.Y.

— International Boundaries of September 1, 1939
— Allied Maritime Supply Routes
The Allies
The Axis Powers
Areas Occupied by the Allies
Areas Occupied by the Axis Powers
Vichy-controlled Areas (later to Allies)
Sphere of German U-boat Operations
Neutral States
Allied Advances

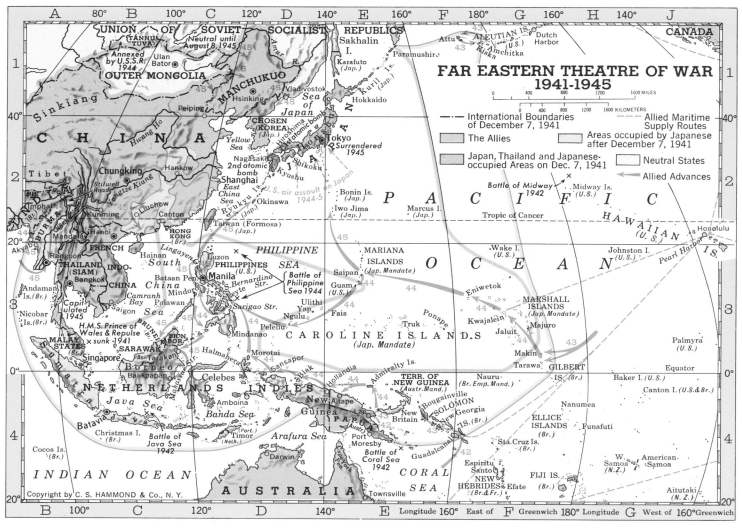

FAR EASTERN THEATRE OF WAR 1941-1945

— International Boundaries of December 7, 1941
— Allied Maritime Supply Routes
The Allies
Areas occupied by Japanese after December 7, 1941
Japan, Thailand and Japanese-occupied Areas on Dec. 7, 1941
Neutral States
Allied Advances

Copyright by C. S. HAMMOND & Co., N.Y.

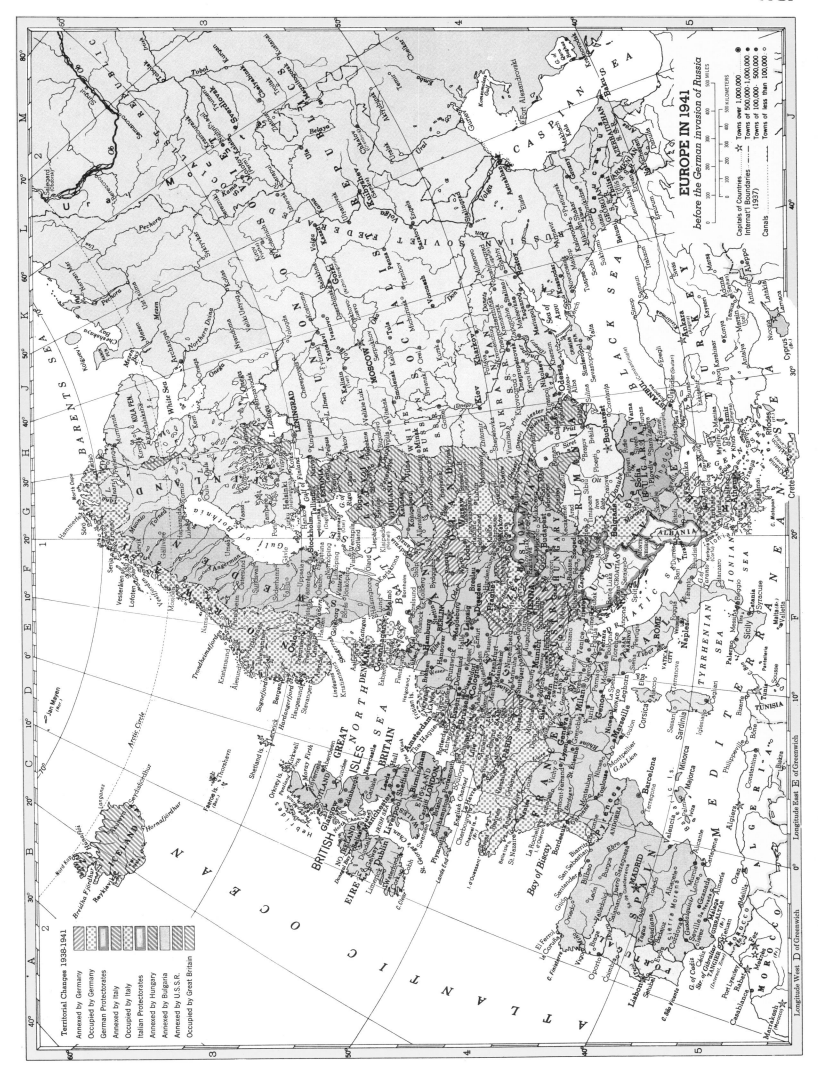

EUROPE IN 1941

before the German invasion of Russia

Territorial Changes 1938-1941

Annexed by Germany
Occupied by Germany
German Protectorates
Annexed by Italy
Occupied by Italy
Italian Protectorates
Annexed by Hungary
Annexed by Bulgaria
Annexed by U.S.S.R.
Occupied by Great Britain

EUROPE DURING THE COLD WAR 1945–1989

Legend:
- ─── The Iron Curtain
- ◆ Members of the North Atlantic Treaty Organization (NATO) Canada and U.S. are also members
- ■ Members of the European Economic Community (EEC)
- ▲ Members of the European Free Trade Association (EFTA)
- ★ Members of the Warsaw Pact

Capitals of Countries ⊙ International Boundaries ───
Internal Boundaries ─────

© Copyright HAMMOND INCORPORATED, Maplewood, N.J.

PRESENT-DAY EUROPE
LAMBERT AZIMUTHAL EQUAL-AREA PROJECTION

NATO and EFTA continue as active organizations. The EEC (EC) became the European Union (EU) in 1994. Since 1989 Sweden, Finland and Austria have become EU members.

Capitals of Countries ⊙ International Boundaries ───
Internal Boundaries ─────

© Copyright HAMMOND INCORPORATED, Maplewood, N.J.

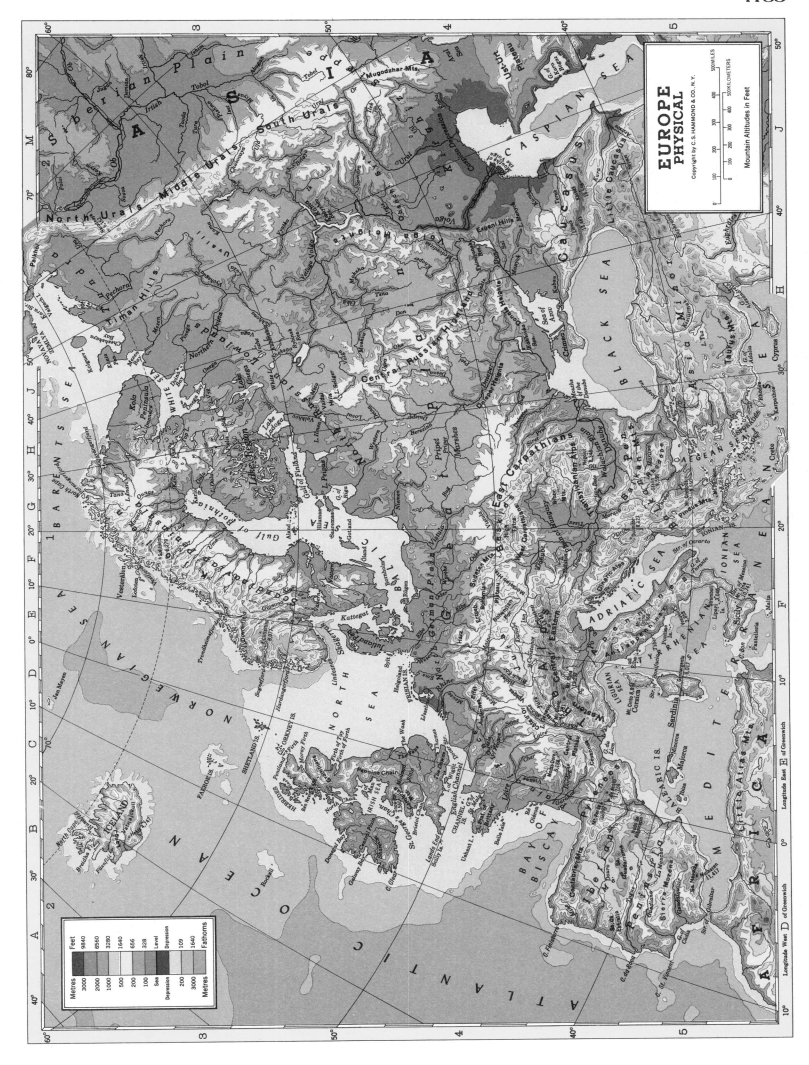

EUROPE
PHYSICAL

Copyright by C. S. HAMMOND & CO., N.Y.

Mountain Altitudes in Feet

Feet	Metres
9840	3000
6560	2000
3280	1000
1640	500
656	200
328	100
Level	Sea
Depression	Depression
109	200
1640	3000
Fathoms	Metres

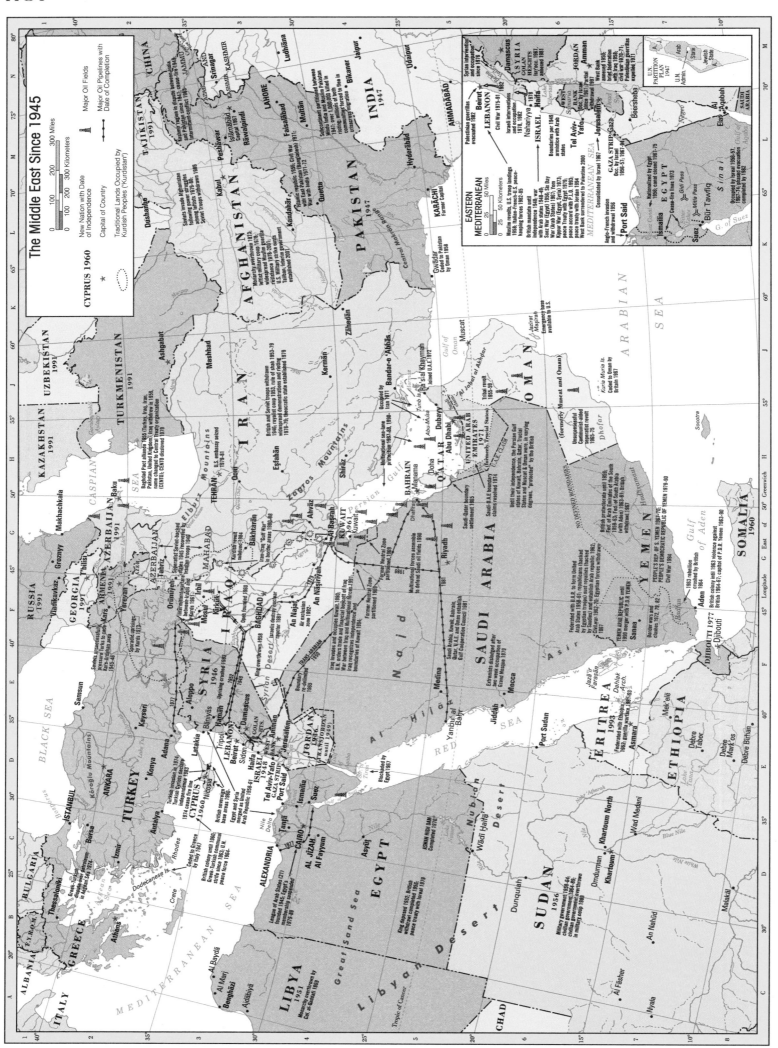

The Middle East Since 1945

CYPRUS 1960

★ New Nation with Date of Independence

★ Capital of Country

Traditional Lands Occupied by Kurdish Peoples ("Kurdistan")

▲ Major Oil Fields

Major Oil Pipelines with Date of Completion

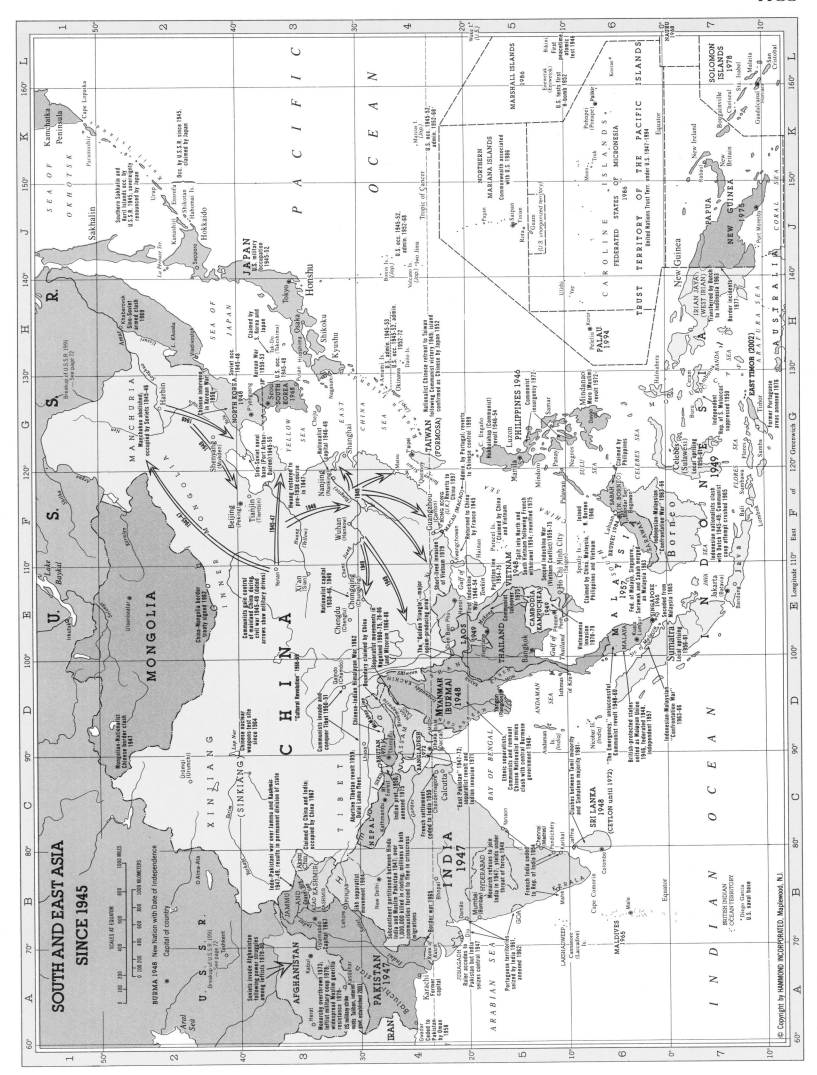

SOUTH AND EAST ASIA SINCE 1945

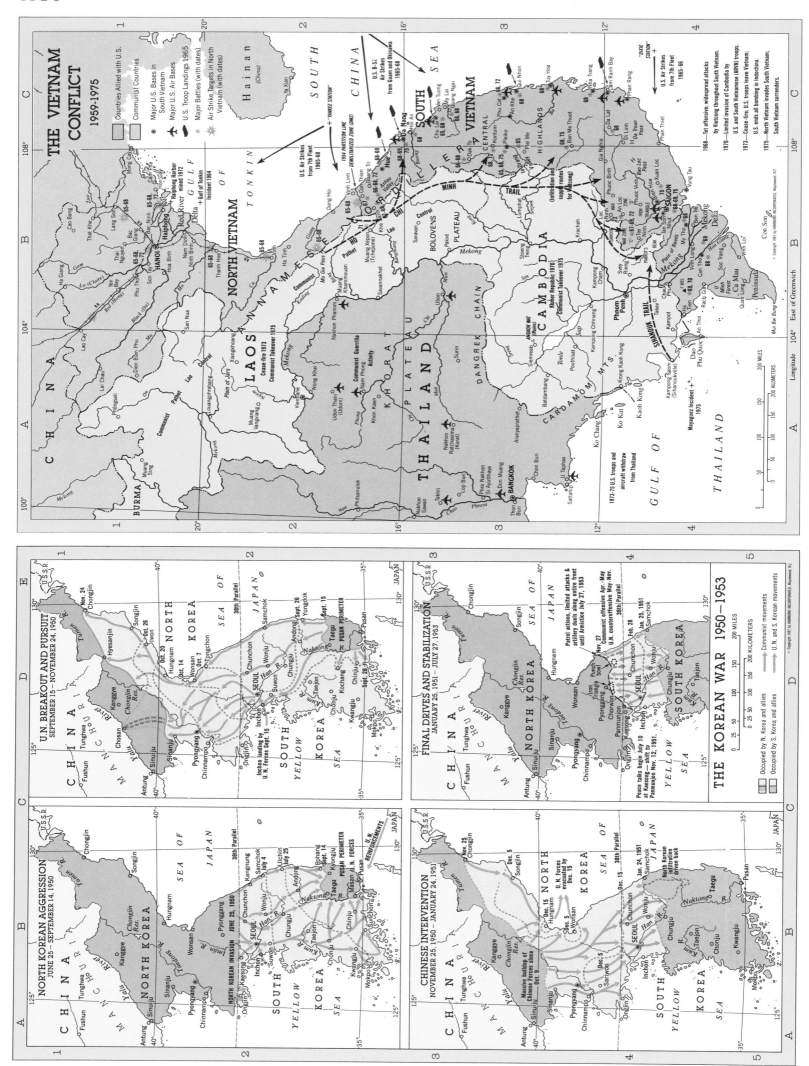

THE VIETNAM CONFLICT
1959-1975

Countries Allied with U.S.
Communist Countries
● Major U.S. Bases in South Vietnam
✈ Major U.S. Air Bases
⚓ U.S. Troop Landings 1965
✳ Major Battles (with dates)
✳ Air Strike Targets in North Vietnam (with dates)

1968—Tet offensive; widespread attacks by Vietcong throughout South Vietnam.
1970—Limited invasion of Cambodia by U.S. and South Vietnamese (ARVN) troops.
1973—Cease-fire; U.S. troops leave Vietnam; U.S. ends all bombing in Indochina.
1975—North Vietnam invades South Vietnam; South Vietnam surrenders.

1973-75 U.S. troops and aircraft withdraw from Thailand

THE KOREAN WAR 1950–1953

NORTH KOREAN AGGRESSION
JUNE 25 – SEPTEMBER 14, 1950

U.N. BREAKOUT AND PURSUIT
SEPTEMBER 15 – NOVEMBER 24, 1950

CHINESE INTERVENTION
NOVEMBER 25, 1950 – JANUARY 24, 1951

FINAL DRIVES AND STABILIZATION
JANUARY 25, 1951 – JULY 27, 1953

Occupied by N. Korea and allies
Occupied by S. Korea and allies

Communist movements
U. N. and S. Korean movements

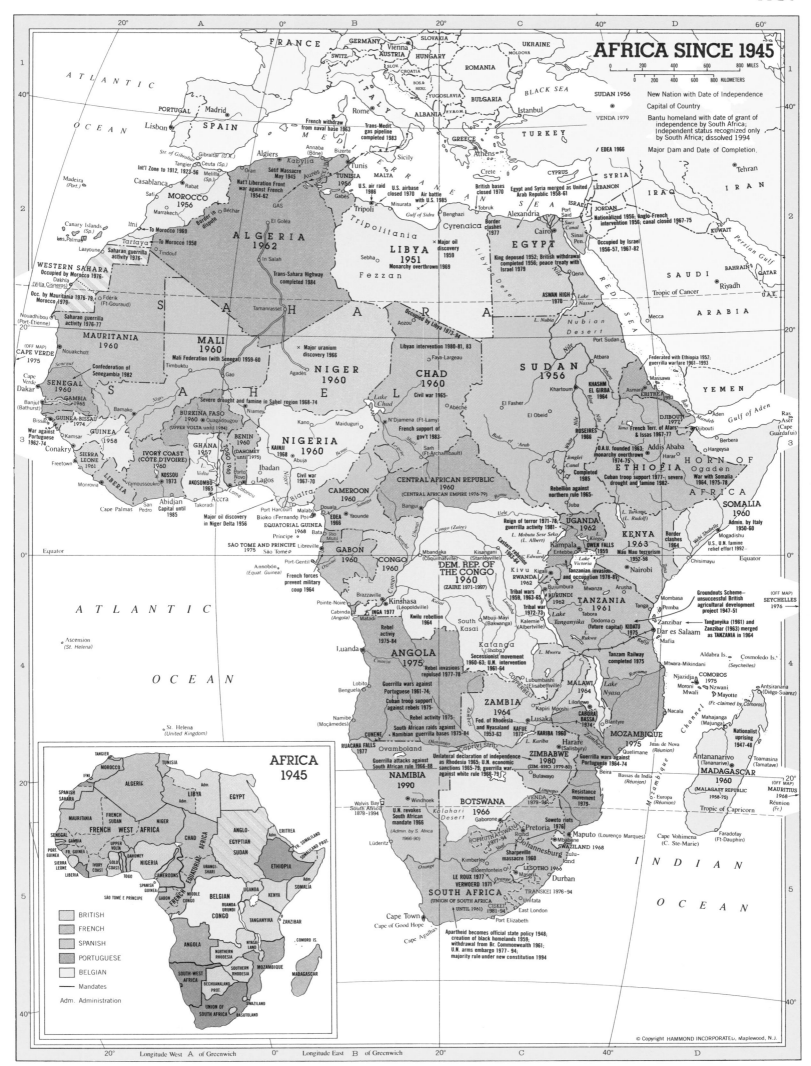

AFRICA SINCE 1945

SUDAN 1956 ⊛ New Nation with Date of Independence

Capital of Country

VENDA 1979 Bantu homeland with date of grant of independence by South Africa; Independent status recognized only by South Africa; dissolved 1994

EDEA 1966 Major Dam and Date of Completion.

AFRICA 1945

BRITISH
FRENCH
SPANISH
PORTUGUESE
BELGIAN
— Mandates
Adm. Administration

© Copyright HAMMOND INCORPORATED, Maplewood, N.J.

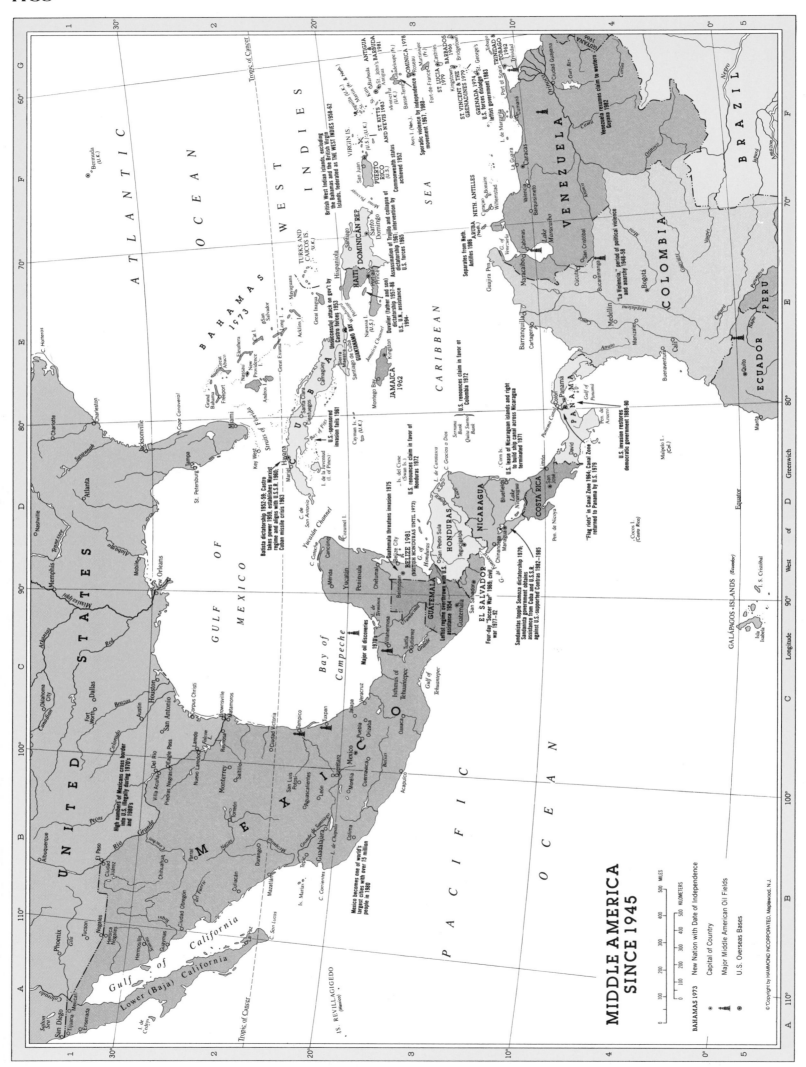

MIDDLE AMERICA
SINCE 1945

BAHAMAS 1973   New Nation with Date of Independence

Capital of Country

Major Middle American Oil Fields

U.S. Overseas Bases

© Copyright by HAMMOND INCORPORATED, Maplewood, N.J.

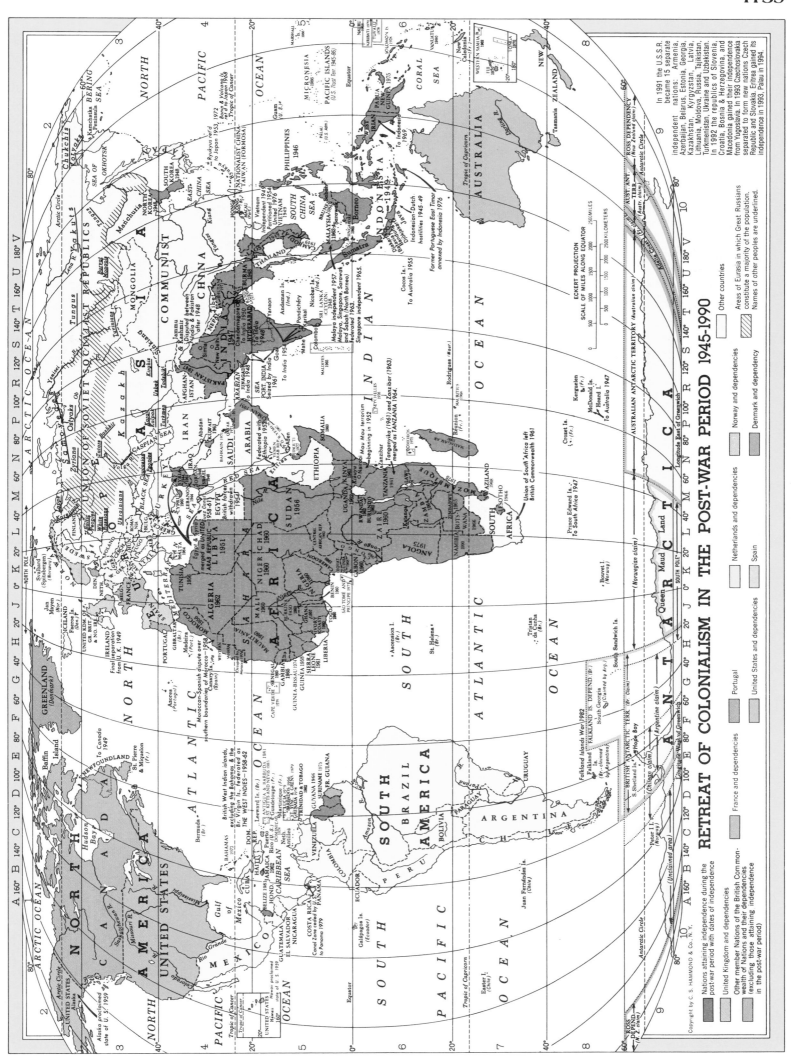

RETREAT OF COLONIALISM IN THE POST-WAR PERIOD 1945-1990

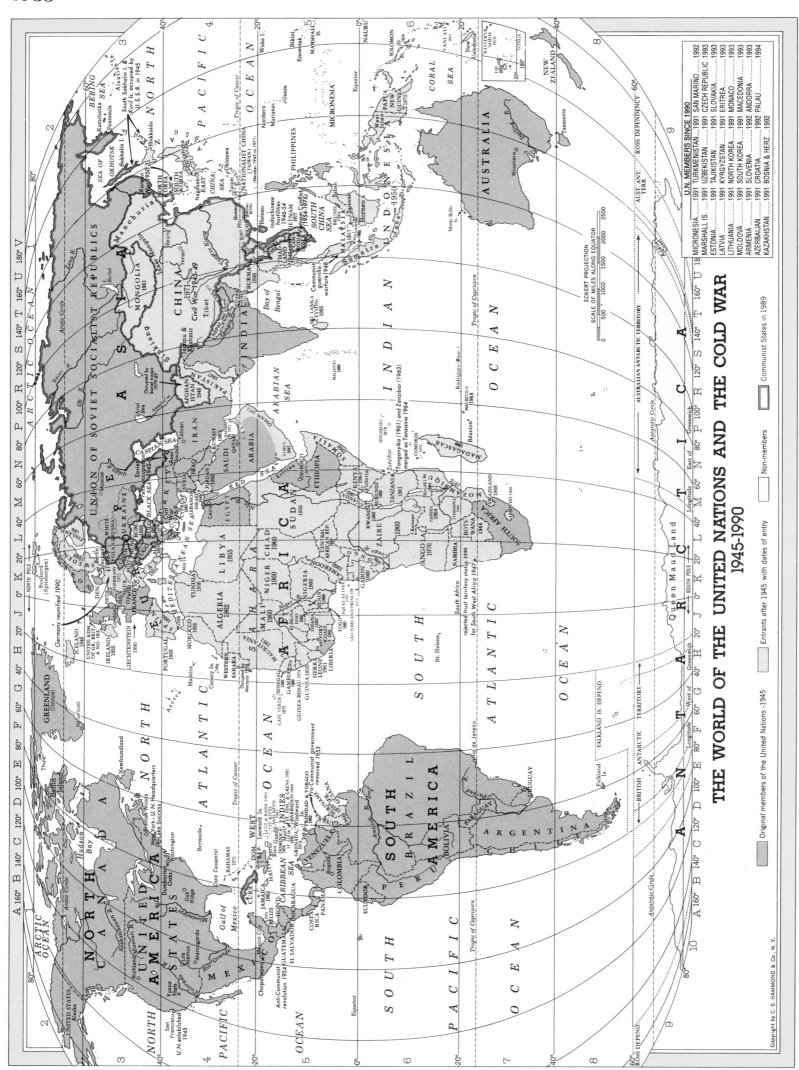

THE WORLD OF THE UNITED NATIONS AND THE COLD WAR
1945-1990

Original members of the United Nations -1945

Entrants after 1945 with dates of entry

Non-members

Communist States in 1989

ECKERT PROJECTION
SCALE OF MILES ALONG EQUATOR
0   500   1000   1500   2000   2500

U.N. MEMBERS SINCE 1990		
MICRONESIA..........1991	TURKMENISTAN..1992	SAN MARINO......1992
MARSHALL IS.........1991	UZBEKISTAN......1992	CZECH REPUBLIC.1993
ESTONIA.............1991	TAJIKISTAN......1992	SLOVAKIA........1993
LATVIA..............1991	KYRGYZSTAN......1992	ERITREA.........1993
LITHUANIA...........1991	NORTH KOREA.....1991	MONACO..........1993
MOLDOVA.............1991	SOUTH KOREA.....1991	MACEDONIA.......1993
ARMENIA.............1991	SLOVENIA........1991	ANDORRA.........1993
AZERBAIJAN..........1991	CROATIA.........1992	PALAU...........1994
KAZAKHSTAN..........1991	BOSNIA & HERZ...1992	

Copyright C. S. HAMMOND & Co., N. Y.

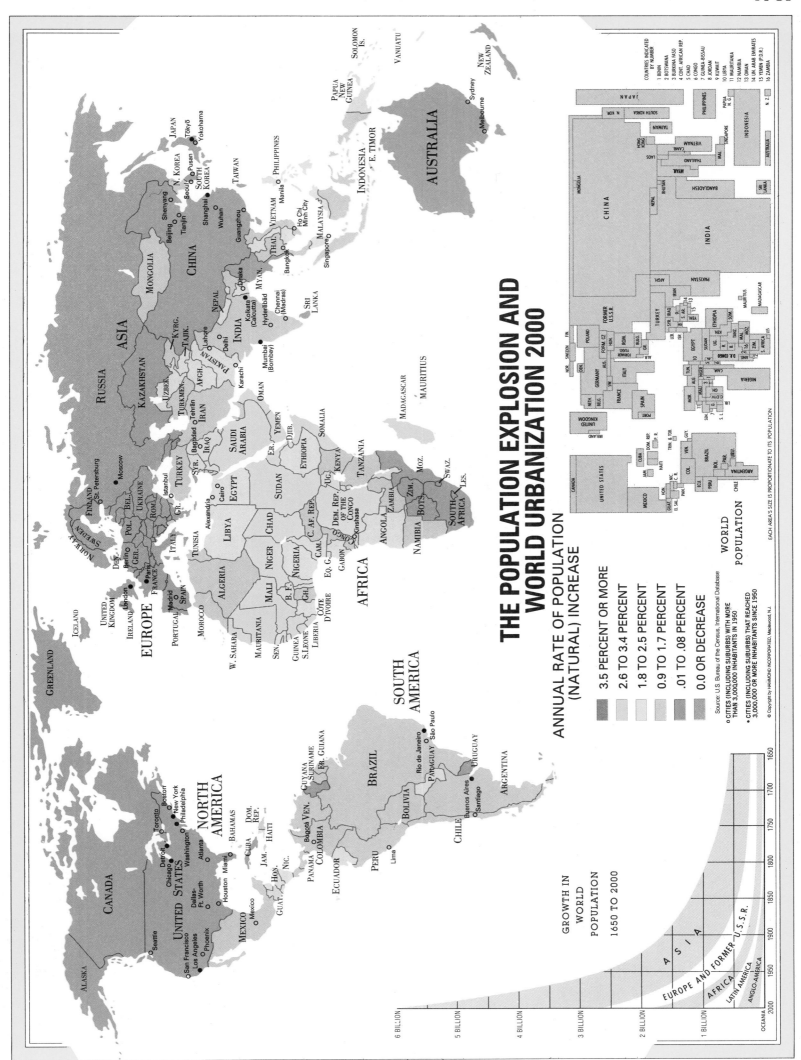

THE POPULATION EXPLOSION AND WORLD URBANIZATION 2000

ANNUAL RATE OF POPULATION (NATURAL) INCREASE

- 3.5 PERCENT OR MORE
- 2.6 TO 3.4 PERCENT
- 1.8 TO 2.5 PERCENT
- 0.9 TO 1.7 PERCENT
- .01 TO .08 PERCENT
- 0.0 OR DECREASE

Source: U.S. Bureau of the Census, International Database

○ CITIES (INCLUDING SUBURBS) WITH MORE THAN 3,000,000 INHABITANTS IN 1950

● CITIES (INCLUDING SUBURBS) THAT REACHED 3,000,000 OR MORE INHABITANTS SINCE 1950

© Copyright by HAMMOND INCORPORATED, Maplewood, N.J.

WORLD POPULATION

EACH AREA'S SIZE IS PROPORTIONAL TO ITS POPULATION

COUNTRIES INDICATED BY NUMBER
1 BENIN
2 BOTSWANA
3 BURKINA FASO
4 CENT. AFRICAN REP.
5 CHAD
6 CONGO
7 GUINEA-BISSAU
8 JORDAN
9 KUWAIT
10 LIBYA
11 MAURITANIA
12 NAMIBIA
13 OMAN
14 UN. ARAB EMIRATES
15 YEMEN (P.D.R.)
16 ZAMBIA

GROWTH IN WORLD POPULATION 1650 TO 2000

ASIA
EUROPE AND FORMER U.S.S.R.
AFRICA
LATIN AMERICA
ANGLO-AMERICA
OCEANIA

1650 1700 1750 1800 1850 1900 1950 2000

6 BILLION
5 BILLION
4 BILLION
3 BILLION
2 BILLION
1 BILLION

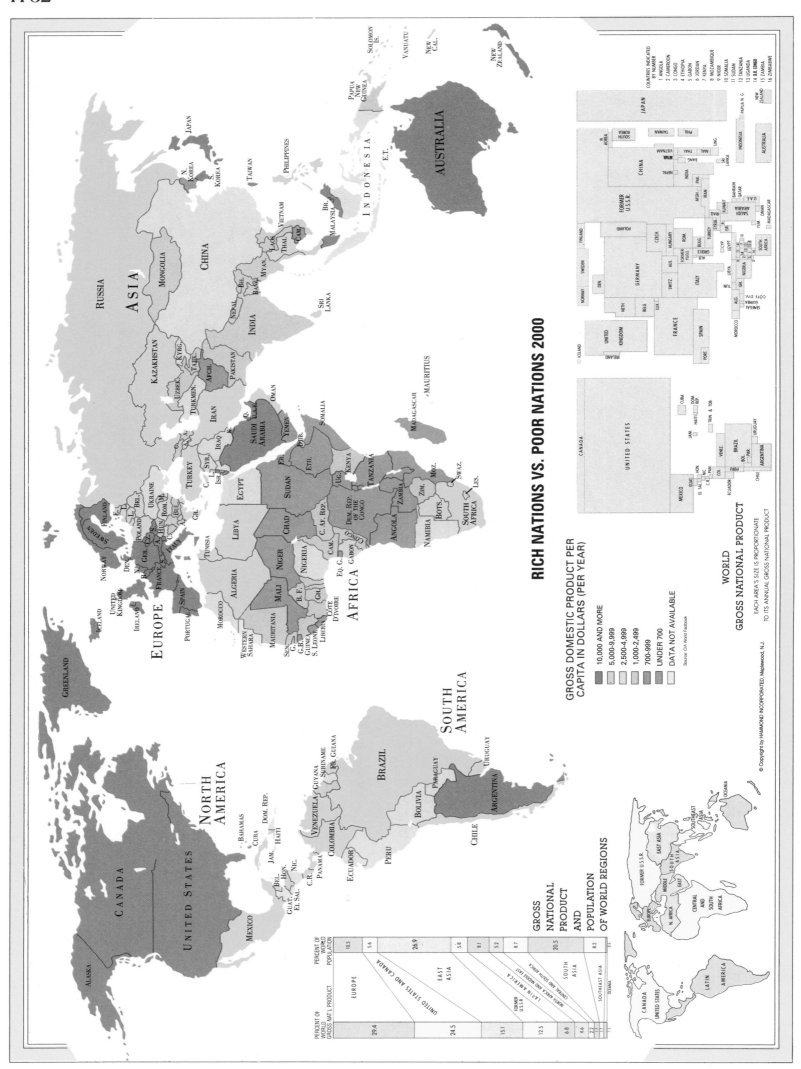

RICH NATIONS VS. POOR NATIONS 2000

GROSS DOMESTIC PRODUCT PER CAPITA IN DOLLARS (PER YEAR)

- 10,000 AND MORE
- 5,000-9,999
- 2,500-4,999
- 1,000-2,499
- 700-999
- UNDER 700
- DATA NOT AVAILABLE

Source: CIA World Factbook

WORLD GROSS NATIONAL PRODUCT

EACH AREA'S SIZE IS PROPORTIONATE TO ITS ANNUAL GROSS NATIONAL PRODUCT

© Copyright by HAMMOND INCORPORATED, Maplewood, N.J.

COUNTRIES INDICATED BY NUMBER
1 ANGOLA
2 CAMEROON
3 CONGO
4 ETHIOPIA
5 GABON
6 JORDAN
7 KENYA
8 MOZAMBIQUE
9 NIGER
10 SOMALIA
11 SUDAN
12 TANZANIA
13 UGANDA
14 D.R. CONGO
15 ZAMBIA
16 ZIMBABWE

GROSS NATIONAL PRODUCT AND POPULATION OF WORLD REGIONS

	PERCENT OF WORLD GROSS NAT'L PRODUCT	PERCENT OF WORLD POPULATION
EUROPE	29.4	10.5
UNITED STATES AND CANADA	24.5	5.6
EAST ASIA	15.1	26.9
FORMER U.S.S.R.	12.5	5.8
LATIN AMERICA	6.8	8.1
NORTH AFRICA AND MIDDLE EAST	4.6	5.2
SOUTH ASIA	2.2	8.7
SOUTHEAST ASIA	1.3	20.5
OCEANIA	1.1	8.2

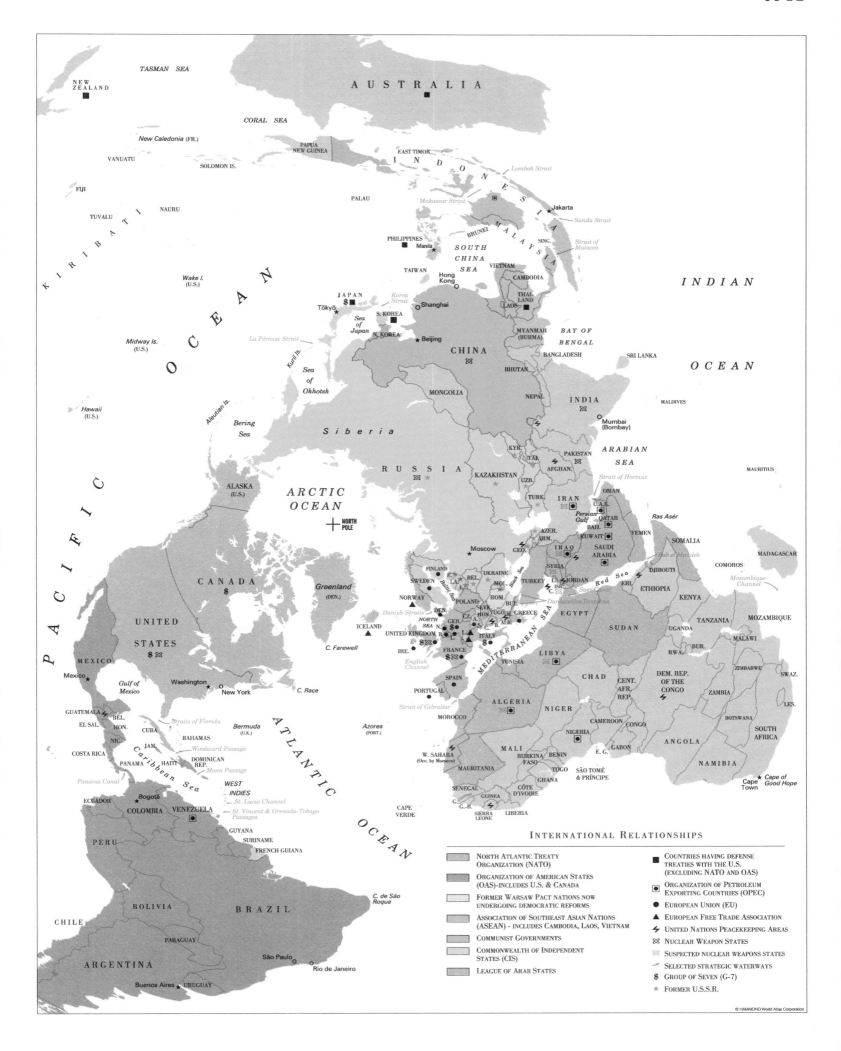

TASMAN SEA

NEW ZEALAND

CORAL SEA

AUSTRALIA

New Caledonia (FR.)

VANUATU

PAPUA NEW GUINEA

EAST TIMOR

I N D O N E S I A

Lombok Strait

FIJI

SOLOMON IS.

Makassar Strait

Jakarta

Sunda Strait

TUVALU

NAURU

PALAU

BRUNEI

MALAYSIA

SING.

Strait of Malacca

K I R I B A T I

Wake I. (U.S.)

PHILIPPINES

Manila

SOUTH CHINA SEA

VIETNAM

CAMBODIA

TAIWAN

Hong Kong

THAI-LAND

INDIAN

JAPAN

Korea Strait

Shanghai

MYANMAR (BURMA)

LAOS

Midway Is. (U.S.)

Tōkyō

Sea of Japan

S. KOREA

N. KOREA

Beijing

CHINA

BAY OF BENGAL

La Pérouse Strait

Kuril Is.

Sea of Okhotsk

MONGOLIA

BHUTAN

BANGLADESH

SRI LANKA

OCEAN

Hawaii (U.S.)

Bering Sea

Siberia

NEPAL

INDIA

MALDIVES

ALASKA (U.S.)

RUSSIA

KAZAKHSTAN

KYR.

TAJ.

PAKISTAN

AFGHAN.

ARABIAN SEA

MAURITIUS

P A C I F I C

Bering Strait

ARCTIC OCEAN

NORTH POLE

UZB.

TURK.

IRAN

OMAN

Strait of Hormuz

U.A.E.

Ras Asēr

QATAR

Persian Gulf

BAH.

KUWAIT

YEMEN

SOMALIA

MADAGASCAR

AZER.

ARM.

IRAQ

SAUDI ARABIA

COMOROS

Moscow

GEO.

SYRIA

Bab el Mandeb

DJIBOUTI

Mozambique Channel

CANADA

Greenland (DEN.)

FINLAND

UKRAINE

TURKEY

JORDAN

Red Sea

ERI.

ETHIOPIA

KENYA

SWEDEN

LA.

BEL.

MOL.

Black Sea

ISR.

L.

Suez Canal

Baltic Sea

NORWAY

POLAND

ROM.

Dardanelles/Bosporus

EGYPT

SUDAN

UGANDA

TANZANIA

MOZAMBIQUE

Danish Straits

DEN.

SVK.

BUL.

GREECE

Mediterranean Sea

UNITED STATES

ICELAND

NORTH SEA

GER.

CZ.

YUGO.

ALB.

LIBYA

MALAWI

MEXICO

UNITED KINGDOM

N.

B.

L.

ITALY

CHAD

CENT. AFR. REP.

DEM. REP. OF THE CONGO

ZAMBIA

ZIMBABWE

SWAZ.

Mexico

Gulf of Mexico

Washington

New York

C. Race

IRE.

FRANCE

TUNISIA

NIGER

CAMEROON

CONGO

ANGOLA

LES.

English Channel

SPAIN

ALGERIA

MALI

GABON

BOTSWANA

SOUTH AFRICA

GUATEMALA

BEL.

HON.

CUBA

Bermuda (U.K.)

PORTUGAL

MOROCCO

BURKINA FASO

BENIN

NIGERIA

E.G.

SÃO TOMÉ & PRÍNCIPE

NAMIBIA

EL SAL.

NIC.

BAHAMAS

Strait of Gibraltar

W. SAHARA (Occ. by Morocco)

TOGO

GHANA

COSTA RICA

JAM.

HAITI

DOMINICAN REP.

Azores (PORT.)

MAURITANIA

SENEGAL

CÔTE D'IVOIRE

Cape Town

Cape of Good Hope

PANAMA

Caribbean Sea

Mona Passage

G.-B.

GUINEA

LIBERIA

Panama Canal

WEST INDIES

St. Lucia Channel

CAPE VERDE

SIERRA LEONE

ECUADOR

Bogotá

St. Vincent & Grenada-Tobago Passages

COLOMBIA

VENEZUELA

GUYANA

SURINAME

FRENCH GUIANA

PERU

A T L A N T I C   O C E A N

BOLIVIA

BRAZIL

C. de São Roque

CHILE

PARAGUAY

São Paulo

ARGENTINA

Rio de Janeiro

Buenos Aires

URUGUAY

© HAMMOND World Atlas Corporation

INTERNATIONAL RELATIONSHIPS

- NORTH ATLANTIC TREATY ORGANIZATION (NATO)
- ORGANIZATION OF AMERICAN STATES (OAS)-INCLUDES U.S. & CANADA
- FORMER WARSAW PACT NATIONS NOW UNDERGOING DEMOCRATIC REFORMS
- ASSOCIATION OF SOUTHEAST ASIAN NATIONS (ASEAN) - INCLUDES CAMBODIA, LAOS, VIETNAM
- COMMUNIST GOVERNMENTS
- COMMONWEALTH OF INDEPENDENT STATES (CIS)
- LEAGUE OF ARAB STATES

- ■ COUNTRIES HAVING DEFENSE TREATIES WITH THE U.S. (EXCLUDING NATO AND OAS)
- ⊡ ORGANIZATION OF PETROLEUM EXPORTING COUNTRIES (OPEC)
- ● EUROPEAN UNION (EU)
- ▲ EUROPEAN FREE TRADE ASSOCIATION
- ⚡ UNITED NATIONS PEACEKEEPING AREAS
- ⌧ NUCLEAR WEAPON STATES
- ⌧ SUSPECTED NUCLEAR WEAPONS STATES
- ⌁ SELECTED STRATEGIC WATERWAYS
- $ GROUP OF SEVEN (G-7)
- ★ FORMER U.S.S.R.

TIME CHART

Columns: DATE | NATIVE AMERICANS | BLACK AFRICANS | NORTH AFRICANS | EGYPTIANS | ARABIANS | IRANIANS | HEBREWS | PHOENICIANS | MESOPOTAMIANS | HITTITES | HELLENES (GREEKS) | AEGEANS

DATE axis (top to bottom): LATE STONE AGE, 5000 B.C., 4000, 3000, 2000 B.C., 1750, 1500, 1250, 1000 B.C.

Well before 6000 B.C. people began to domesticate animals, and to gather and store grains and other crops in the Near East, Pakistan, the Americas, and China. Gradually, improved techniques of food production—the sowing of seed, cultivation and irrigation—were developed. Populations increased, trade in pottery and craft skills began, and new types of society and technology were possible.

The first use of copper metal occurred around 4000 B.C. in Anatolia and Iran.

NATIVE AMERICANS:
- Clovis and Folsom big-game hunters in N. America
- Manioc and high altitude grains in S. America
- Domestication of llama, alpaca in Andes
- Maize cultivated in Mexico
- First pottery in Americas
- Cotton cultivated in Peru
- Arctic Small Tool culture
- Early Pueblo culture in N. Amer.
- First metalwork in Peru
- Olmec civilization 1200-900
- Mayas enter Cent. Amer.

BLACK AFRICANS:
- A-Group Nubian culture at Qustul
- Hunter-gatherers in West and Central Africa

NORTH AFRICANS:
- Mixed ancestral threads in Africa north of Sahara
- Saharan pottery
- Nubian and S. African rock painting
- Cattle domesticated
- Nubia invaded by Eygpt
- Utica founded by Phoenicians
- Libyan dynasty

EGYPTIANS:
- Settled Egyptian communities in Nile Valley with Nubian, Saharan & Armenoid linkages
- Badarian culture
- Naqada I
- Predynasty Lower and Upper Kdms.
- Naqada II
- Egyptian hieroglyphics
- Menes unifies Egypt c. 2900
- OLD KDM. 2685-2180
- Pyramid Age
- 1st Intermediate period
- MIDDLE KDM. 2040-1786
- Hyksos invaders
- 2nd Intermediate period
- NEW KINGDOM 1570-1070
- Thutmose III
- Ikhnaton
- Invasion of Sea Peoples
- Rameses II
- 3rd Intermediate period 1070-712
- EGYPT

ARABIANS:
- Minaean Kdm.

IRANIANS:
- Elamite civilization emerges
- ELAM
- Wars with Babylon
- Golden Age of Elam

HEBREWS:
- Abraham
- Exodus c. 1290
- Conquest of Canaan
- David
- Solomon

PHOENICIANS:
- Phoenicians occupy coastal areas
- Extensive Mediterranean trade
- Egyptian rule
- Hiram of Tyre

MESOPOTAMIANS:
- Extensive farming in Mesopotamia
- Earliest irrigation system c.5500
- Early communities in the Tigris-Euphrates Valley
- Growth of Sumerian cities
- Cuneiform writing
- 1st dynasty of Ur
- Sargon I Akkadian dynasty
- BABYLONIA / ASSYRIA
- OLD BABYLONIAN EMPIRE
- Hammurabi c. 1700
- Mitanni Kdm.
- ASSYRIA
- BABYLONIA
- Kassite rule
- Shalmaneser I
- Tiglath-pileser I
- Aramaean invasion

HITTITES:
- Early Hittite Kingdoms
- Labarnas est. Empire c. 1700
- HITTITE EMPIRE
- Iron weapons introduced
- Battle of Kadesh 1296
- Hittites driven from Asia Minor

HELLENES (GREEKS):
- Migration of Greek-speaking peoples
- Aeolian & Achaean invasions
- Mycenae
- Ionian invasion
- Trojan War c. 1190
- Dorian invasion
- Local aristocracies

AEGEANS:
- MINOAN CIVILIZATION
- Palace at Knossos
- Height of Cretan culture
- Fall of Crete 1400

ANCIENT EMPIRES map:
HITTITE KDM., ASSYRIA, BABYLONIAN EMP., EGYPTIAN KDM.
ANCIENT EMPIRES
— Assyrian Empire 7th Cent. B.C.

A Graphic History of Mankind

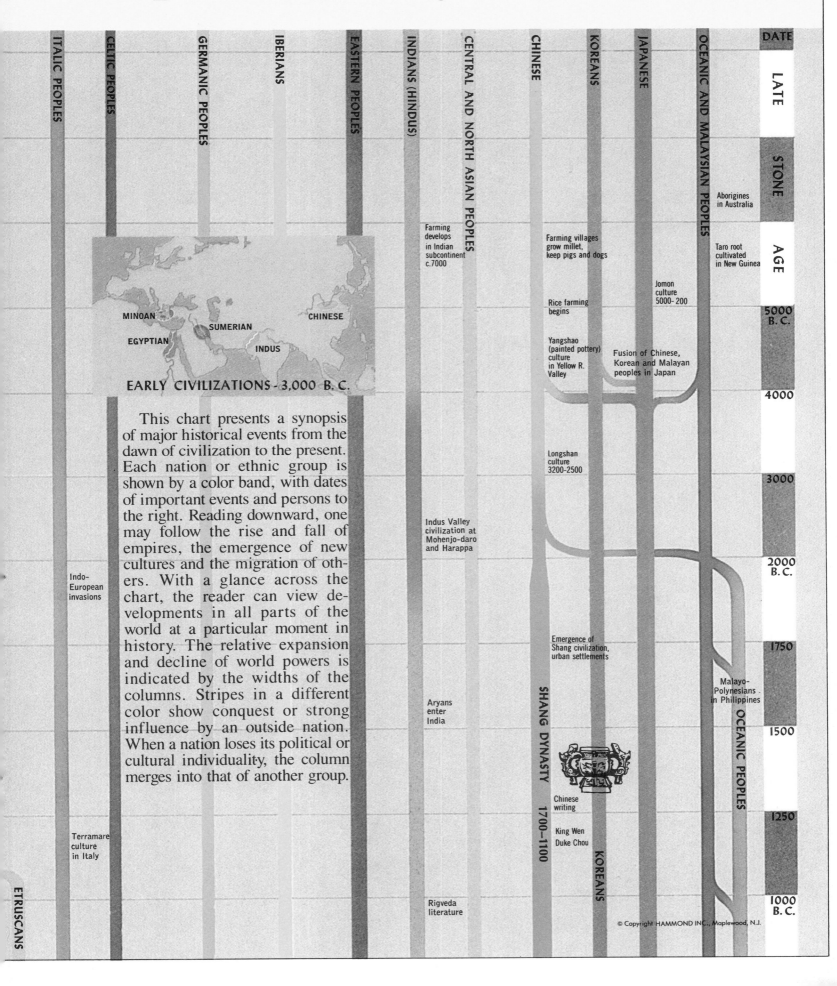

ITALIC PEOPLES

CELTIC PEOPLES

GERMANIC PEOPLES

IBERIANS

EASTERN PEOPLES

INDIANS (HINDUS)

CENTRAL AND NORTH ASIAN PEOPLES

CHINESE

KOREANS

JAPANESE

OCEANIC AND MALAYSIAN PEOPLES

DATE

LATE

STONE

AGE

5000 B.C.

4000

3000

2000 B.C.

1750

1500

1250

1000 B.C.

EARLY CIVILIZATIONS - 3,000 B.C.

MINOAN
EGYPTIAN
SUMERIAN
INDUS
CHINESE

This chart presents a synopsis of major historical events from the dawn of civilization to the present. Each nation or ethnic group is shown by a color band, with dates of important events and persons to the right. Reading downward, one may follow the rise and fall of empires, the emergence of new cultures and the migration of others. With a glance across the chart, the reader can view developments in all parts of the world at a particular moment in history. The relative expansion and decline of world powers is indicated by the widths of the columns. Stripes in a different color show conquest or strong influence by an outside nation. When a nation loses its political or cultural individuality, the column merges into that of another group.

Indo-European invasions

Terramare culture in Italy

ETRUSCANS

Farming develops in Indian subcontinent c.7000

Indus Valley civilization at Mohenjo-daro and Harappa

Aryans enter India

Rigveda literature

Farming villages grow millet, keep pigs and dogs

Rice farming begins

Yangshao (painted pottery) culture in Yellow R. Valley

Longshan culture 3200-2500

Emergence of Shang civilization, urban settlements

SHANG DYNASTY 1700-1100

Chinese writing

King Wen Duke Chou

Jomon culture 5000- 200

Fusion of Chinese, Korean and Malayan peoples in Japan

KOREANS

Aborigines in Australia

Taro root cultivated in New Guinea

Malayo-Polynesians in Philippines

OCEANIC PEOPLES

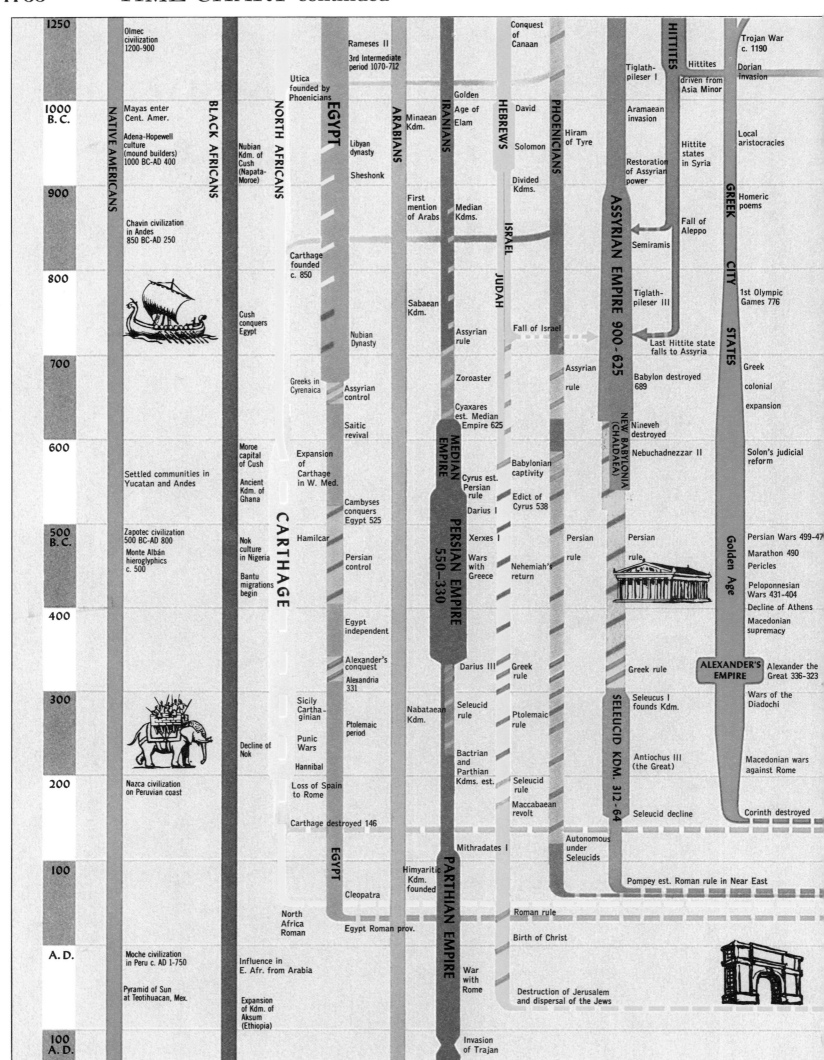

1250	NATIVE AMERICANS	Olmec civilization 1200-900	BLACK AFRICANS	NORTH AFRICANS	EGYPT	Utica founded by Phoenicians	Rameses II / 3rd Intermediate period 1070-712	ARABIANS	IRANIANS	Golden Age of Elam	HEBREWS	Conquest of Canaan	HITTITES	Tiglath-pileser I	Hittites driven from Asia Minor	GREEK CITY STATES	Trojan War c. 1190 / Dorian invasion
1000 B.C.		Mayas enter Cent. Amer. / Adena-Hopewell culture (mound builders) 1000 BC-AD 400		Nubian Kdm. of Cush (Napata-Moroe)		Libyan dynasty / Sheshonk		Minaean Kdm.		David / Solomon		Hiram of Tyre / PHOENICIANS	Aramaean invasion	Hittite states in Syria		Homeric poems / Local aristocracies
900						First mention of Arabs	Median Kdms.		Divided Kdms.			Restoration of Assyrian power	Fall of Aleppo		
800		Chavin civilization in Andes 850 BC-AD 250		Cush conquers Egypt		Carthage founded c. 850	Sabaean Kdm.		ISRAEL / JUDAH			ASSYRIAN EMPIRE 900-625	Semiramis / Tiglath-pileser III		1st Olympic Games 776
700						Nubian Dynasty / Greeks in Cyrenaica	Assyrian control	Assyrian rule	Fall of Israel		Assyrian rule	Last Hittite state falls to Assyria / Babylon destroyed 689		Greek colonial expansion
600		Settled communities in Yucatan and Andes		Moroe capital of Cush / Ancient Kdm. of Ghana		Saitic revival / Expansion of Carthage in W. Med.	Zoroaster / Cyaxares est. Median Empire 625	MEDIAN EMPIRE	Babylonian captivity		NEW BABYLONIA (CHALDAEA)	Nineveh destroyed / Nebuchadnezzar II		Solon's judicial reform
500 B.C.		Zapotec civilization 500 BC-AD 800 / Monte Albán hieroglyphics c. 500		Nok culture in Nigeria / Bantu migrations begin	CARTHAGE	Cambyses conquers Egypt 525 / Hamilcar / Persian control	Cyrus est. Persian rule / Darius I / Xerxes I / Wars with Greece	PERSIAN EMPIRE 550-330	Edict of Cyrus 538 / Nehemiah's return	Persian rule	Persian rule		Golden Age	Persian Wars 499-47 / Marathon 490 / Pericles / Peloponnesian Wars 431-404 / Decline of Athens
400						Egypt independent / Alexander's conquest / Alexandria 331		Darius III	Greek rule	Greek rule		ALEXANDER'S EMPIRE	Macedonian supremacy / Alexander the Great 336-323
300				Decline of Nok		Sicily Cartha-ginian / Punic Wars / Hannibal / Ptolemaic period	Nabataean Kdm.	Seleucid rule	Ptolemaic rule	Seleucus I founds Kdm.	SELEUCID KDM. 312-64		Wars of the Diadochi
200		Nazca civilization on Peruvian coast				Loss of Spain to Rome	Bactrian and Parthian Kdms. est.	Seleucid rule / Maccabaean revolt	Antiochus III (the Great)		Macedonian wars against Rome
100					EGYPT	Carthage destroyed 146 / Cleopatra	Mithradates I / Himyaritic Kdm. founded	PARTHIAN EMPIRE	Seleucid decline / Autonomous under Seleucids / Pompey est. Roman rule in Near East		Corinth destroyed
A.D.		Moche civilization in Peru c. AD 1-750 / Pyramid of Sun at Teotihuacan, Mex.		North Africa Roman		Egypt Roman prov.		Roman rule / Birth of Christ		
100 A.D.				Influence in E. Afr. from Arabia / Expansion of Kdm. of Aksum (Ethiopia)			War with Rome / Invasion of Trajan	Destruction of Jerusalem and dispersal of the Jews		

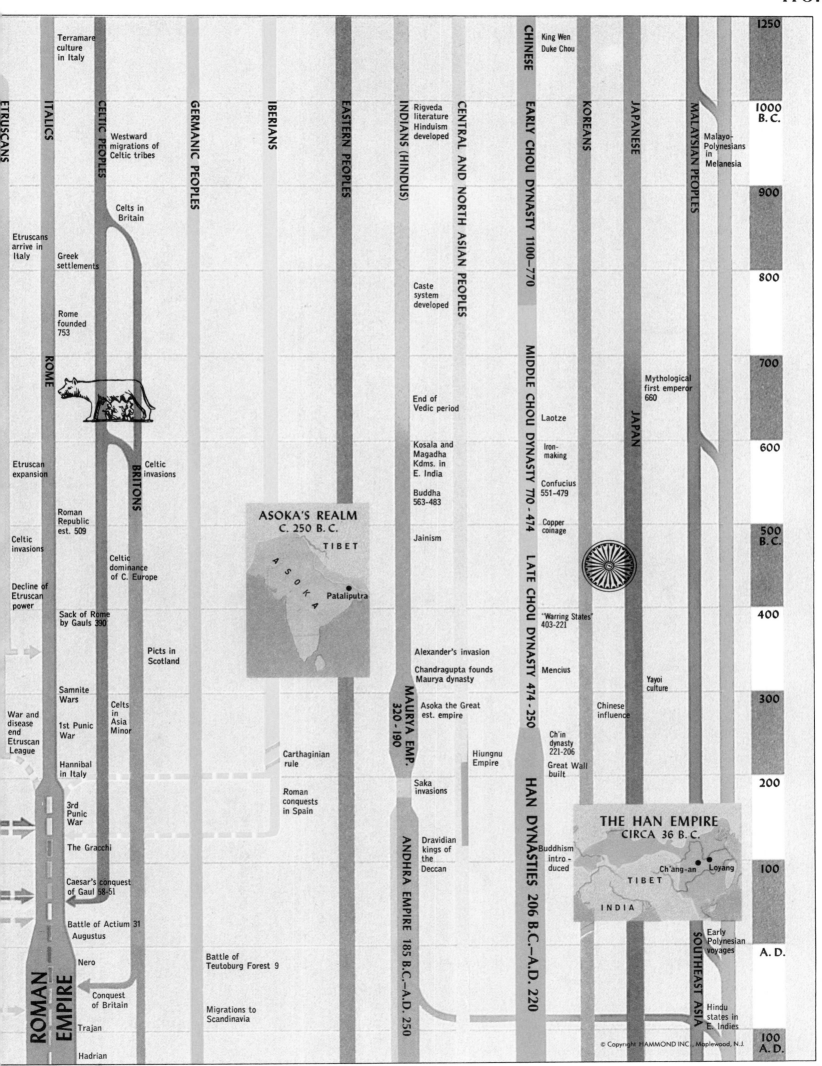

ETRUSCANS

ITALICS

CELTIC PEOPLES

GERMANIC PEOPLES

IBERIANS

EASTERN PEOPLES

INDIANS (HINDUS)

CENTRAL AND NORTH ASIAN PEOPLES

EARLY CHOU DYNASTY 1100-770

KOREANS

JAPANESE

MALAYSIAN PEOPLES

1250

1000 B.C.

900

800

700

600

500 B.C.

400

300

200

100

A.D.

100 A.D.

Terramare culture in Italy

Etruscans arrive in Italy

Etruscan expansion

Celtic invasions

Decline of Etruscan power

War and disease end Etruscan League

Rome founded 753

ROME

Roman Republic est. 509

Sack of Rome by Gauls 390

Samnite Wars

1st Punic War

Hannibal in Italy

3rd Punic War

The Gracchi

Caesar's conquest of Gaul 58-51

Battle of Actium 31
Augustus

Nero

ROMAN EMPIRE

Conquest of Britain

Trajan

Hadrian

Westward migrations of Celtic tribes

Celts in Britain

Greek settlements

BRITONS

Celtic invasions

Celtic dominance of C. Europe

Picts in Scotland

Celts in Asia Minor

Battle of Teutoburg Forest 9

Migrations to Scandinavia

Carthaginian rule

Roman conquests in Spain

Rigveda literature Hinduism developed

Caste system developed

End of Vedic period

Kosala and Magadha Kdms. in E. India

Buddha 563-483

Jainism

ASOKA'S REALM C. 250 B.C.

TIBET

ASOKA

Pataliputra

Alexander's invasion

Chandragupta founds Maurya dynasty

MAURYA EMP. 320-190

Asoka the Great est. empire

Saka invasions

ANDHRA EMPIRE 185 B.C.—A.D. 250

Dravidian kings of the Deccan

Hiungnu Empire

King Wen
Duke Chou

MIDDLE CHOU DYNASTY 770-474

Laotze

Iron-making

Confucius 551-479

Copper coinage

LATE CHOU DYNASTY 474-250

"Warring States" 403-221

Mencius

Ch'in dynasty 221-206

Great Wall built

HAN DYNASTIES 206 B.C.—A.D. 220

Buddhism intro-duced

THE HAN EMPIRE CIRCA 36 B.C.

Ch'ang-an   Loyang

TIBET

INDIA

JAPAN

Mythological first emperor 660

Chinese influence

Yayoi culture

Malayo-Polynesians in Melanesia

SOUTHEAST ASIA

Early Polynesian voyages

Hindu states in E. Indies

© Copyright HAMMOND INC., Maplewood, N.J.

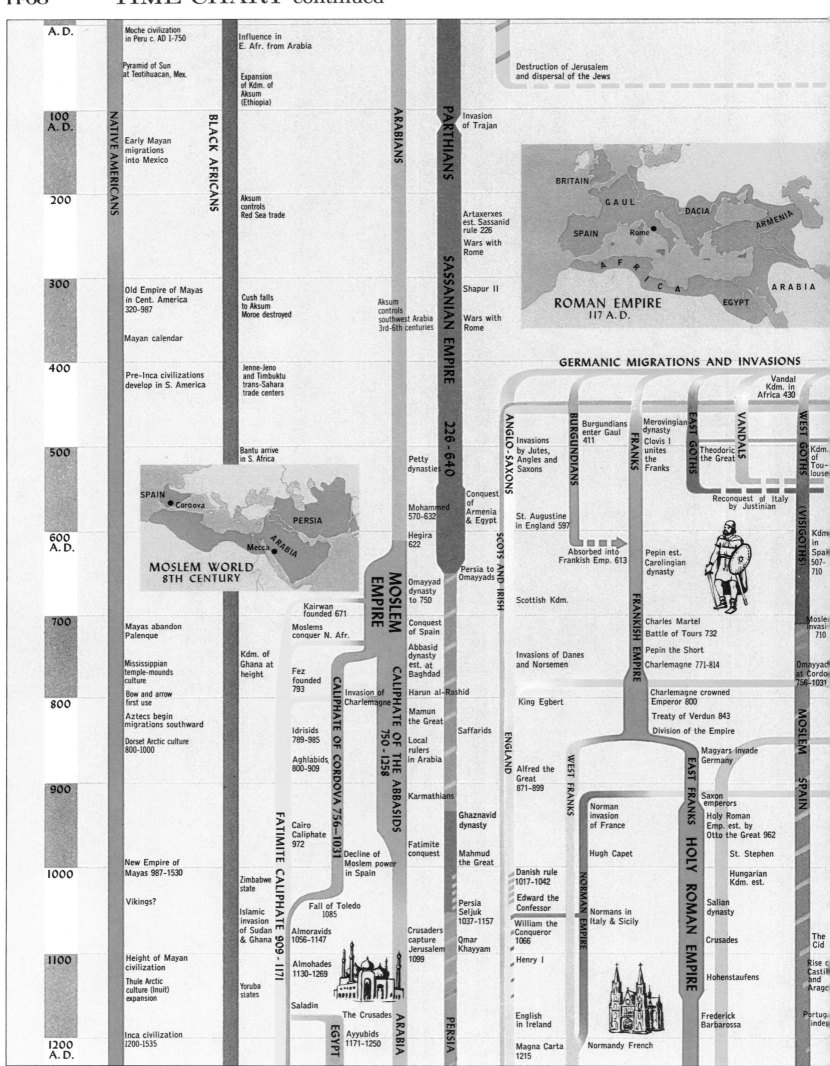

A.D.	NATIVE AMERICANS	BLACK AFRICANS		ARABIANS	PARTHIANS							
	Moche civilization in Peru c. AD 1-750	Influence in E. Afr. from Arabia										
	Pyramid of Sun at Teotihuacan, Mex.	Expansion of Kdm. of Aksum (Ethiopia)					Destruction of Jerusalem and dispersal of the Jews					
100 A.D.	Early Mayan migrations into Mexico					Invasion of Trajan						
200		Aksum controls Red Sea trade			SASSANIAN EMPIRE 226-640	Artaxerxes est. Sassanid rule 226		**ROMAN EMPIRE 117 A.D.**				
						Wars with Rome						
300	Old Empire of Mayas in Cent. America 320-987	Cush falls to Aksum Moroe destroyed		Aksum controls southwest Arabia 3rd-6th centuries		Shapur II						
	Mayan calendar					Wars with Rome						
400	Pre-Inca civilizations develop in S. America	Jenne-Jeno and Timbuktu trans-Sahara trade centers						**GERMANIC MIGRATIONS AND INVASIONS**				
500	Bantu arrive in S. Africa			Petty dynasties			ANGLO-SAXONS	BURGUNDIANS	Burgundians enter Gaul 411	FRANKS	EAST GOTHS	VANDALS	WEST GOTHS (VISIGOTHS)
	MOSLEM WORLD 8TH CENTURY			Conquest of Armenia & Egypt		Invasions by Jutes, Angles and Saxons		Merovingian dynasty Clovis I unites the Franks	Theodoric the Great	Vandal Kdm. in Africa 430		
600 A.D.			MOSLEM EMPIRE	Mohammed 570-632		St. Augustine in England 597			Reconquest of Italy by Justinian			
				Hegira 622		SCOTS AND IRISH	Absorbed into Frankish Emp. 613	Pepin est. Carolingian dynasty			Kdm. of Tou-louse	
				Omayyad dynasty to 750	Persia to Omayyads	Scottish Kdm.					Kdm. in Spain 507-710	
700	Mayas abandon Palenque	Kdm. of Ghana at height	Kairwan founded 671	Conquest of Spain			FRANKISH EMPIRE	Charles Martel Battle of Tours 732				Moslem invasion 710
	Mississippian temple-mounds culture	Moslems conquer N. Afr.	CALIPHATE OF CORDOVA 756-1031	Abbasid dynasty est. at Baghdad	CALIPHATE OF THE ABBASIDS 750-1258	Invasions of Danes and Norsemen		Pepin the Short Charlemagne 771-814				Omayyad at Cordo 756-1031
800	Bow and arrow first use	Fez founded 793	Invasion of Charlemagne	Harun al-Rashid		King Egbert		Charlemagne crowned Emperor 800				MOSLEM SPAIN
	Aztecs begin migrations southward	Idrisids 789-985		Mamun the Great			ENGLAND	Treaty of Verdun 843 Division of the Empire				
	Dorset Arctic culture 800-1000	Aghlabids 800-909		Local rulers in Arabia	Saffarids				Magyars invade Germany			
900			FATIMITE CALIPHATE 909-1171	Karmathians		Alfred the Great 871-899	WEST FRANKS	Norman invasion of France	Saxon emperors Holy Roman Emp. est. by Otto the Great 962	EAST FRANKS	HOLY ROMAN EMPIRE	
	New Empire of Mayas 987-1530	Cairo Caliphate 972		Ghaznavid dynasty				Hugh Capet	St. Stephen			
1000	Vikings?	Zimbabwe state	Decline of Moslem power in Spain	Fatimite conquest Mahmud the Great		Danish rule 1017-1042	NORMAN EMPIRE		Hungarian Kdm. est. Salian dynasty			
		Islamic invasion of Sudan & Ghana	Fall of Toledo 1085		Persia Seljuk 1037-1157	Edward the Confessor		Normans in Italy & Sicily				The Cid
1100	Height of Mayan civilization	Almoravids 1056-1147		Crusaders capture Jerusalem 1099	Qmar Khayyam	William the Conqueror 1066		Crusades				Rise o Castil and Arago
	Thule Arctic culture (Inuit) expansion	Almohades 1130-1269 Yoruba states				Henry I		Hohenstaufens				
1200 A.D.	Inca civilization 1200-1535	Saladin	EGYPT	The Crusades Ayyubids 1171-1250	ARABIA	English in Ireland Magna Carta 1215	PERSIA	Normandy French	Frederick Barbarossa			Portuga indep

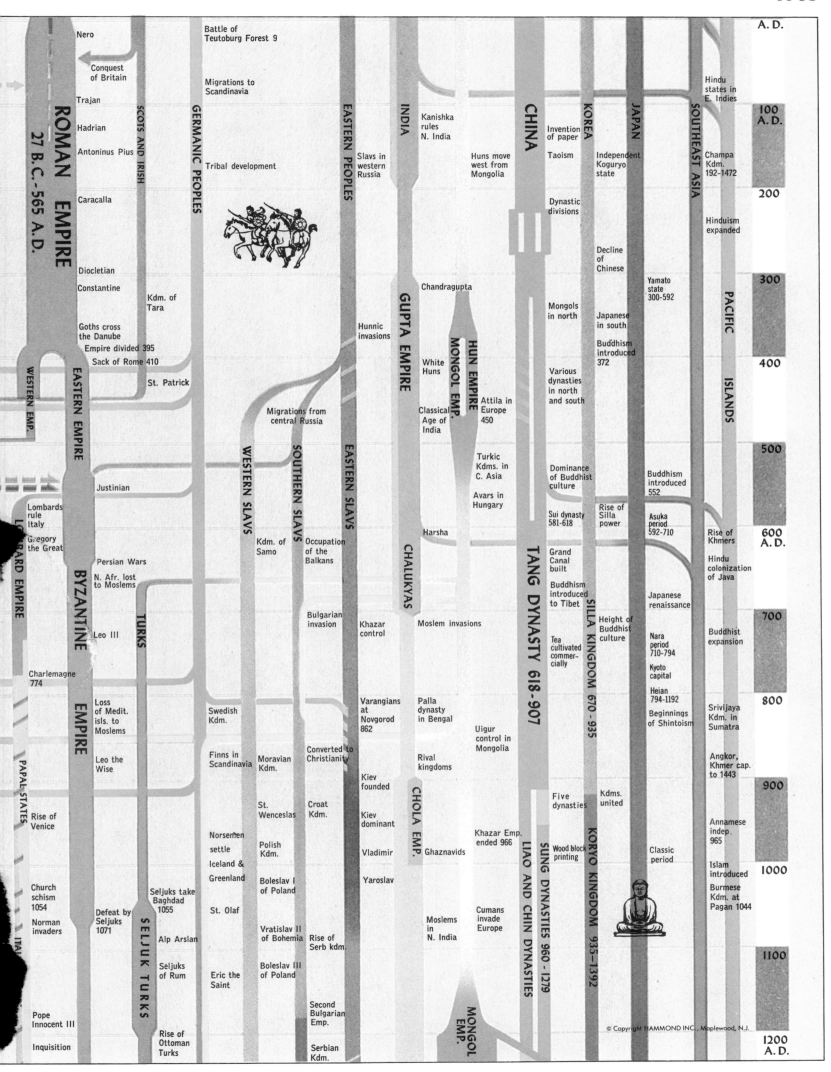

A.D.

ROMAN EMPIRE 27 B.C.–565 A.D.

Nero

Conquest of Britain

Trajan

Hadrian

Antoninus Pius

Caracalla

Diocletian

Constantine

SCOTS AND IRISH

Kdm. of Tara

Goths cross the Danube

Empire divided 395

Sack of Rome 410

St. Patrick

WESTERN EMP.

EASTERN EMPIRE

Justinian

Lombards rule Italy

Gregory the Great

Persian Wars

N. Afr. lost to Moslems

BYZANTINE EMPIRE

Leo III

Charlemagne 774

Loss of Medit. isls. to Moslems

Leo the Wise

LOMBARD EMPIRE

PAPAL STATES

Rise of Venice

Church schism 1054

Norman invaders

TURKS

Seljuks take Baghdad 1055

Defeat by Seljuks 1071

Alp Arslan

Seljuks of Rum

SELJUK TURKS

Pope Innocent III

Inquisition

Rise of Ottoman Turks

GERMANIC PEOPLES

Battle of Teutoburg Forest 9

Migrations to Scandinavia

Tribal development

Migrations from central Russia

WESTERN SLAVS

Kdm. of Samo

Swedish Kdm.

Finns in Scandinavia

Moravian Kdm.

Norsemen settle Iceland & Greenland

St. Olaf

Eric the Saint

SOUTHERN SLAVS

Occupation of the Balkans

Bulgarian invasion

Converted to Christianity

St. Wenceslas

Croat Kdm.

Polish Kdm.

Boleslav I of Poland

Vratislav II of Bohemia

Boleslav III of Poland

Rise of Serb kdm.

Second Bulgarian Emp.

Serbian Kdm.

EASTERN PEOPLES

Slavs in western Russia

EASTERN SLAVS

Hunnic invasions

Khazar control

Varangians at Novgorod 862

Kiev founded

Kiev dominant

Vladimir

Yaroslav

Moslems in N. India

INDIA

Kanishka rules N. India

Chandragupta

GUPTA EMPIRE

White Huns

Classical Age of India

Harsha

CHALUKYAS

CHOLA EMP.

HUN EMPIRE / MONGOL EMP.

Attila in Europe 450

Turkic Kdms. in C. Asia

Avars in Hungary

Moslem invasions

Palla dynasty in Bengal

Rival kingdoms

Ghaznavids

MONGOL EMP.

CHINA

Invention of paper

Taoism

Huns move west from Mongolia

Dynastic divisions

Mongols in north

Various dynasties in north and south

Dominance of Buddhist culture

Sui dynasty 581–618

Grand Canal built

Buddhism introduced to Tibet

Tea cultivated commercially

TANG DYNASTY 618–907

Uigur control in Mongolia

Five dynasties

Khazar Emp. ended 966

Wood block printing

LIAO AND CHIN DYNASTIES

SUNG DYNASTIES 960–1279

Cumans invade Europe

KOREA

Independent Koguryo state

Decline of Chinese

Buddhism introduced 372

Rise of Silla power

SILLA KINGDOM 670–935

Height of Buddhist culture

Kdms. united

KORYO KINGDOM 935–1392

JAPAN

Yamato state 300–592

Japanese in south

Buddhism introduced 552

Asuka period 592–710

Japanese renaissance

Nara period 710–794

Kyoto capital

Heian 794–1192

Beginnings of Shintoism

Classic period

SOUTHEAST ASIA

Hindu states in E. Indies

Champa Kdm. 192–1472

Hinduism expanded

PACIFIC ISLANDS

Rise of Khmers

Hindu colonization of Java

Buddhist expansion

Srivijaya Kdm. in Sumatra

Angkor, Khmer cap. to 1443

Annamese indep. 965

Islam introduced

Burmese Kdm. at Pagan 1044

A.D.
100 A.D.
200
300
400
500
600 A.D.
700
800
900
1000
1100
1200 A.D.

© Copyright HAMMOND INC., Maplewood, N.J.

Time scale (left axis): 1200 A.D., 1300, 1400, 1500, 1600, 1700 A.D., 1800, 1850, 1900, 1925, 1950, 1975

NATIVE AMERICANS

Inca civilization 1200-1535

Aztecs found Mexico City c. 1325

Collapse of Pueblo cultures

Destruction of Mayan cities in Yucatan

Height of Inca Emp. c. 1480

Columbus 1492

Cortez conquers Mexico

Pizarro conquers Peru

St. Augustine 1565

Portuguese in Brazil

Jamestown 1607

Champlain

Quebec 1608

Great Plains tribes adopt horse culture

League of the Iroquois

Plains of Abraham 1759

French & Indian War

American Revolution 1775-1783

Louisiana Purchase

War of 1812

Mechanical reaper

Mexican War 1848

First oil well

Civil War 1861-1865

Removal of Indian tribes 1820-1840

LATIN AMERICA

Latin American states indep.

Confederation 1867

Maximilian 1863-1867

Panama Canal opened 1914

Chaco War 1932-1935

Peron in Argentina

Castro in Cuba

Sandinistas in Nicaragua

Falklands War 1982

CANADA

UNITED STATES OF AMERICA

Plymouth 1620

New Amsterdam 1626

La Salle

Statute of Westminster 1931

U.S. enters W.W. I 1917

Women's suffrage 1920

Pearl Harbor W.W. II

Atomic Bomb U.N. founded Korean War 1950-1953

50 states

Civil Rights movement Moon landings Watergate

New Constitution 1982

Trade deficit Persian Gulf crisis

New Province (Nunavut) 1999

BLACK AFRICANS

Mali & Bornu Kdms.

Kdm. of Benin emerges

Baguirmi Kdm.

Great Zimbabwe built

Swahili emporiums

Kongo Kdm.

Portuguese in West Africa

Morocco indep. to 1912

Songhoy Kdm.

Benin declines

Buganda Kdm.

Slave trade

Ashanti Kdm.

Oyo Emp.

European coastal colonies

Liberia independent

Shaka's Zulu Kdm.

End of slave trade

Diamond rush 1870

European colonial expansion

Italians in Libya

Ger. col's to Brit., France & Belg.

Kdm. established

Brit. prot. ended 1936

New African nations

South African apartheid

Portugal gives up colonies 1979

Namibia indep. 1990

First S. Afr. multi-racial election 1994

NORTH AFRICAN STATES

COLONIAL NORTH AFRICA

Hafsids 1228-1534

Portuguese & Sp. in N. Afr.

Turkish rule 1517

Turkish rule in N. Afr.

First Fr. influence in N. Afr.

Fr. in Algeria

Fr. in Tunisia

Suez Canal 1859-1869

Brit. control 1882

Indep. N. Afr.

Algerian War

Qaddafi in Libya

Suez Crisis 1956

Nasser 1954-1970

Sadat 1970-1981

EGYPT

Ayyubids 1171-1250

Mameluke rule 1250-1517

ARABIA

ARABIAN STATES

Portuguese in Oman

Turkish coastal control

Decline of Turkish control

Wahhabis control hinterland

Napoleon in Egypt 1798

Mohammed Ali

Saudi Arabia created

Persian Gulf oil

State of Israel 1948

ISRAEL

Six-day War 1967

OPEC oil embargo 1973

Yom Kippur War 1973

Civil war in Lebanon

Multinational forces free Kuwait 1991

Eritrea Indep. 1993

PERSIA

IRAN

Conquest by Mongol Il-Khans 1256-1336

Moslem restoration

Timurids

Safavid dynasty 1499-1736

Abbas the Great

Nadir Shah

Kajar dynasty

Caucasus area lost to Russia

Persian Revolution

Oil developments

Revolt against Turkey

Mohammed Reza Pahlavi 1941-1979

Khomeini Iran-Iraq War 1980-1988

ENGLAND

SCOTS AND IRISH

GREAT BRITAIN

IRELAND (UNITED KINGDOM)

Magna Carta 1215

Hundred Years War with France 1339-1453

Chaucer

War of the Roses

Tudors

Exploration of America

Henry VIII

Elizabeth I

Spanish Armada destroyed 1588

Shakespeare

Stuarts

Cromwell

Wm. of Orange

Union of Eng. & Scot. 1707

Hanoverians

Treaty of Paris 1763

Beginning of Industrial Revolution

Waterloo 1815

Victoria 1837-1901

Crimean War 1854-1856

Boer War 1899-1902

World War I 1914-1918

Irish Free State est. 1921

De Valera

World War II 1939-1945

Churchill 1940-1945

Colonial withdrawal

Elizabeth II

Sectarian violence in Northern Ireland

Thatcher

European Economic Community (Common Market)

European Union (EU) formed 1999

FRANCE

NAPOLEON'S EMPIRE

Normandy French

Popes at Avignon 1305-1378

Joan of Arc burned 1431

Louis XI

Francis I

Religious Wars

Louis XIV

Louis XV

French Revolution 1789

NAPOLEON'S EMPIRE 1804-1815

Second Republic

Louis Napoleon

Franco-Prussian War

Third Rep.

Ger. invasion & occ.

de Gaulle

HOLY ROMAN EMPIRE

GERMAN STATES

GERMANY

Frederick Hohenzollern

Martin Luther

First Hapsburg Emp.

Charles V

Calvin

Wm. of Orange

Thirty Years War 1618-1648

Turks besiege Vienna 1683

Frederick of Prussia

Frederick II (the Great)

Germanic Confederation

German Emp. 1871

World War I 1914-1918

Defeat of Germany & Austria

Rep.

Rise of Hitler & Nazis 1933

World War II 1939-1945

Divided Germany

Berlin crises

E. Ger. Communist govt. & Berlin Wall fall 1989

Reunification of Germany 1990

HUNGARY

Mongol invasion

Hanseatic League

Union with Poland

John Hunyadi

Indep. from Sp. Hapsburgs 1581

Hungary incorp.

Maria Theresa

AUSTRIA

Metternich chancellor

Dual Monarchy 1867

Franz Josef

Ger. invasion & occ.

Allied occupation

Hung. revolt 1956

Communists lose power

Admitted to NATO 1999

NETHERLANDS AND BELGIUM

BENELUX

Battle of Mohacs 1526

Turkish siege of Vienna

United Provinces 1579-1795

Batavian rep.

Low Countries independent

Congo Free State to Belg.

Wilhelmina Q. of Neth.

Albert I K. of Belg.

Rep.

German invasion & occ.

CHRISTIAN SPAIN

SPAIN AND PORTUGAL

Henry the Navigator

Ferdinand & Isabella

New World Empires

Charles

Philip

Carlist War

First Rep. 1873-1874

Sp. Amer. War

Second Rep.

Civil War

Franco 1936-1975

Sp. Constit. monar. 1975

Napoleon in Spain 1798

Portuguese Kdm.

EMPIRE OF GENGHIS KHAN

ARABIA · TURKESTAN · MONGOLIA · PERSIA · TIBET · INDIA

ITALIAN STATES	BYZANTINE GREEKS		WESTERN SLAVS	SCANDINAVIA	SOUTHERN SLAVS	EASTERN SLAVS	RUSSIAN EMPIRE	INDIA MOGUL EMPIRE	MONGOL EMPIRE KHANATE OF THE GOLDEN HORDE	TATAR EMPIRE 1368-1409	MING DYNASTY 1368-1644 MANCHU (CH'ING) DYNASTY 1644-1912	KOREA	JAPAN ASHIKAGA SHOGUNATE 1333-1573 TOKUGAWA SHOGUNATE 1600-1868	SOUTHEAST ASIA	PACIFIC ISLANDS	
Inquisition	Crusaders take Constantinople 1204	Rise of Ottoman Turks			Serbian Kdm.	Kievan Rus era ends		Sult. of Delhi	Genghis Khan 1206-1227	Chu Shi Neo-Confucianism Kublai Khan	Mongol invasions	Feudal Kamakura period 1192-1333			**1200 A.D.**
Rise of Genoa	Palaeologi 1261-1453									Marco Polo in China		Mongol invasions	Thai migrations		
Dante										Growth of Moslems Christian missionaries	Korean renaissance	Civil wars Rise of the shoguns	Maoris to N.Z.		**1300**
Height of Venetian sea power								Timur sacks Delhi	Timur (Tamerlane)				Thai Kdm. at Ayutthaya 1350-1767		
Great Schism 1378-1417		Mohammed I	Union of Kalmar	Hussite Wars	Turkish control of Balkans	End of Mongol control				Yi dynasty (to 20th century)	Onin War	Decline of Khmers			**1400**
Medici	Turks take Constantinople 1453	Mohammed the Conqueror				Ivan the Great		Vasco da Gama at Calicut 1498					Fall of Madjapahit Kdm. in Java		
da Vinci		Suleiman the Magnificent	Finland to Sweden	Poland and Lithuania united		Ivan the Terrible		Sikh religion founded Akbar the Great	Volga Khanates lost to Russia	Portuguese in Canton & Macao		First Portuguese visit	Burma united		**1500**
			Battle of Lepanto 1571	Livonian War				East India Company 1600		Japanese invasions	St. Francis Xavier Edo 1603-1867	Magellan 1521		
Galileo		Vienna besieged 1683	Gustavus Adolphus	Hapsburgs in Bohemia	Austrian invasion	Romanov dynasty 1613-1917		Aurangzeb 1658-1707		Manchu occupation 1637	Tokyo capital		Dutch found Batavia 1619		**1600**
			John Sobieski	Bohemia to Austria		Peter the Great									**1700 A.D.**
			Charles XII	Polish partitions		Catharine the Great	Clive 1725-1774	Manchu conquest		Tibet conquered 1750		Captain James Cook		
		Russo-Turkish wars		Polish Kdm. under Russia						Christianity introduced	Decline of Shogunate	Thai Kdm. at Bangkok		**1800**
Napoleon's conquests	Greek War of indep. 1821-1830	Battle of Navarino 1827	Finland to Russia 1809	Serb uprising	Napoleon's invasion		British convicts to Australia 1788 Aborigines move inland			Opium wars			Raffles founds Singapore 1819		
Mazzini	Otto I			First Polish Revolution	Balkans auton.	Afghan war	New Zealand colonized 1840							
War of indep.			Second Polish Revolution		Crimean War 1854-1856	Sepoy Rebellion 1857	N.Z.-Maori wars Gold strikes	Taiping Rebellion 1850-1864	Perry's visit 1854			**1850**
Garibaldi	George I									Korea opened to West 1876	Meiji Restoration 1868-1912	French & Brit. protectorates	
Cavour unifies Italy 1861	Modern Olympic Games 1896	Russo-Turkish War 1877		Bulgaria & Serbia indep.	Central Asian expansion	Dominion status to Austr. & N.Z.		Sino-Japanese War 1894-1895			
Kdm. of Italy 1870		Young Turk movement	Norway separate		Russo-Japanese War 1904-1905		World War I	Boxer Rebellion 1900 Sun Yat-sen, Rep. 1912	Annexed by Japan 1910	Russo-Japanese War 1904-1905		**1900**
Italo-Turkish War 1911-1912	Balkan Wars	World War I	Finland indep. 1918	Pilsudski	Balkan Wars	World War I Russian Revolution 1917					World War I 1914	
Mussolini comes to power 1922	Republic	Atatürk forms rep.		Slavic states independent		U.S.S.R. formed 1922	Gandhi's passive resistance 1920's-1948					**1925**
Abyssinia attacked 1935	Kdm. restored 1935		German occ. of Denmark & Norway	German control of Poland & Czech.	German control in Balkans	Stalin 1926-1953 World War II German invasion	World War II	Manchukuo Japanese	Hirohito (Showa) 1926-1989	
World War II	German invasion & occ.			Holocaust Soviet satellites		Indep. of India, Pakistan & Ceylon (Sri Lanka)	ANZUS Treaty 1951	Communist China 1948	Divided Korea	World War II	Fr.-Indochina War
Rep.	Civil War 1944-1950	Turks invade Cyprus 1974		Tito in Yugoslavia 1945-1980		Cold War with West Sputnik 1957	Border clash with China 1962 Bangladesh 1971	Mao Tse-tung Cultural Revolution	Korean War 1950-1953		Indep. of S.E. Asian States	**1950**
	Military dictatorship 1967-1974 Republic 1975			Soviets invade Czechoslovakia 1968		Soviet occupation of Afghanistan 1979-1989	Sikh separatism	Border clashes with U.S.S.R. U.S. recognizes Communist China 1979		Economic prosperity	Vietnam Conflict 1959-1975	**1975**
		Kurdish Conflict 1993		Polish Solidarity movement Communists lose power in E. Europe 1989			Kashmir Conflict 1999	N.Z. bans nuclear ships & weapons	Economic reforms Pro-democracy protests crushed 1989	Government scandals	New Pacific nations
				Poland admitted to NATO 1999	Breakup of Yugoslavia, 1992 Czech Rep. 1993 Kosovo Conflict 1999	Breakup of Soviet Union 1991			Hong Kong to China 1997	Akihito	

© Copyright HAMMOND INC., Maplewood, N.J.

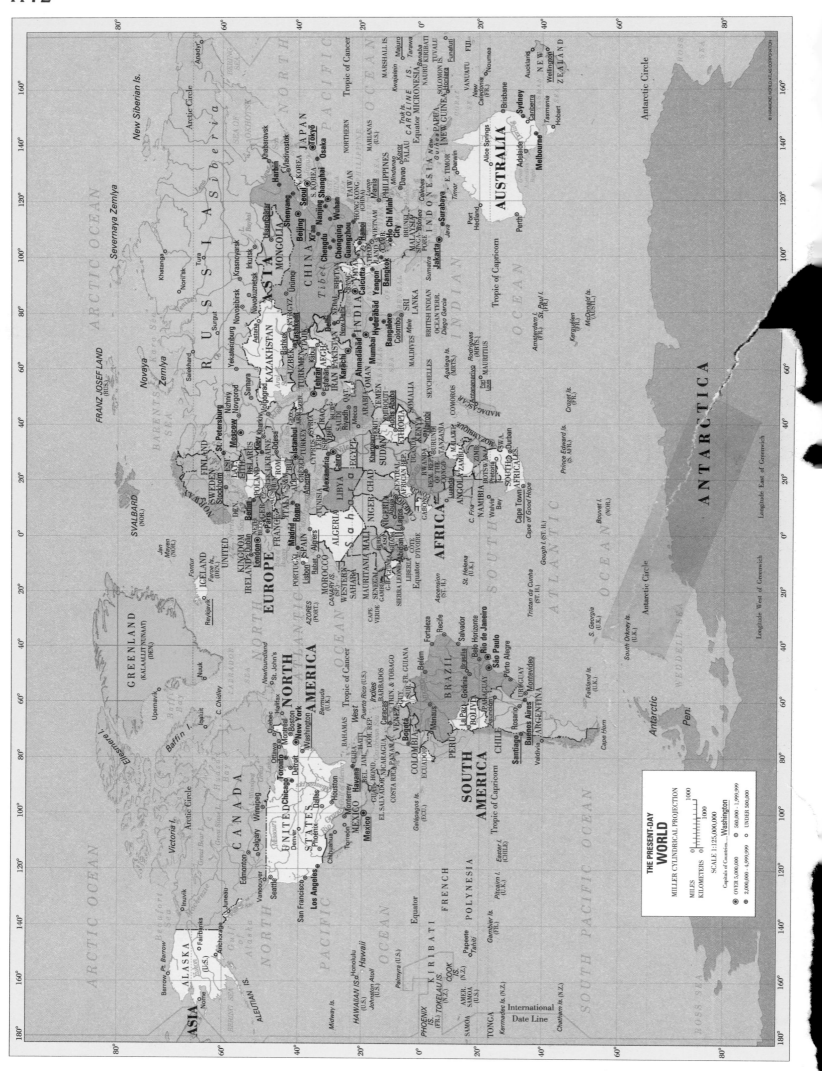

THE PRESENT-DAY
WORLD
MILLER CYLINDRICAL PROJECTION

SCALE 1:125,000,000

Capitals of Countries........Washington

MILES

KILOMETERS

● OVER 5,000,000 ● 500,000 - 1,999,999
⊙ 2,000,000 - 4,999,999 ○ UNDER 500,000